OCCUPATIONAL SAFETY
AND HEALTH SERIES
No. 51

STRESS IN INDUSTRY

CAUSES, EFFECTS AND PREVENTION

L. Levi

INTERNATIONAL LABOUR OFFICE GENEVA

ISBN 92-2-103539-5
ISSN 0078-3129

First published 1984

Printed by the International Labour Office, Geneva, Switzerland

PREFACE

Countless people in today's society complain of "stress". The word is often misused, and used, in the most varied of meanings.

What, then, do we actually mean by stress? How does it feel? What takes place in the body? Does it make sense to talk about stress illnesses? How common are they? Can stress be measured? Can stress be cured or, indeed, can it be prevented?

In the following pages an attempt is made to answer both these and other common questions about stress. To facilitate comprehension, a few simplifications have been unavoidable. The aim has been merely to present the most elementary of introductions. Those who wish, therefore, to explore the topic more thoroughly are referred to the more detailed works listed in the bibliography at the end of this booklet.

The Swedish research on which this book is partly based was supported by grants to the author from the Swedish Work Environment Fund, the Swedish Medical Research Council (Contract No. 4316), the Swedish Delegation for Social Research, Ministry of Social Affairs, the Swedish Delegation for Applied Medical Defence Research, the Folksam Insurance Group, Stockholm, and the Bank of Sweden Tercentenary Fund.

The text evolved, in part, from earlier papers authored or coauthored by the present author. Principal references are: L. Levi: *Stress* (Stockholm, Skandia Insurance Co., 1983); L. Levi, M. Frankenhaeuser and G. Gardell: "Work stress related to social structures and processes", in G.R. Elliott and C. Eisdorfer (eds.): *Stress and human health* (New York, Springer, 1982); L. Levi: *Preventing work stress* (Reading, Massachusetts, Addison-Wesley, 1981); and L. Levi: "Prevention of stress-related disorders on a population scale", in *International Journal of Mental Health*, Vol. 9, 1981, No. 1-2, pp. 9-26. The publishers' permission to quote from these texts is gratefully acknowledged.

I wish to express my gratitude to my colleagues Drs. N. Gavrilescu and A.R. Kagan for constructive criticism and much valuable information.

Last but not least, I should like to express my indebtedness to Mrs. Gun Nerje, who dealt skilfully and patiently with the manuscript through its many revisions.

Lennart Levi,
Laboratory for Clinical Stress Research/
WHO Psychological Centre,
Karokinska Institute,
Stockholm, Sweden

CONTENTS

vi

———————

STRESS

1

What is stress?

In the language of engineering, stress is a force which deforms bodies. In biology and medicine, the term has acquired another sense (cf. Levi, 1971). It refers to a process in the body, to the body's general plan for adapting to all the influences, changes, demands and strains to which it might be exposed. This plan swings into action, for example, when a person is attacked in the street, but also when someone is exposed to radioactivity or to extreme heat or cold. But it is not just _physical_ strains which activate this plan; _mental_ and _social_ ones do so as well - for instance, when we are reminded of an unpleasant experience or are expected to achieve something of which we do not believe we are capable, or when, with or without cause, we worry about our job or family life.

There is something common to all these cases in the way the body attempts to adapt. This common denominator (Selye, 1971), this _stereotype_ - a kind of "revving up" or stepping on the gas - is stress. Stress is, then, a stereotype in the body's responses to, generally speaking, influences, demands or strains. Sometimes these reactions are pleasant, sometimes unpleasant; sometimes useful, sometimes doing harm - but always the same. Some level of stress is _always_ to be found in the body, just as, to draw a rough parallel, a country maintains a certain state of preparedness even in peace-time. Occasionally, this preparedness is intensified, sometimes with good cause, at other times not.

In this way the stress level affects the rate at which processes of _wear and tear_ in the body take place. The more "gas" is given, the higher the speed at which the body's engine is driven, the more quickly the "fuel" is used up, and the more rapidly the "engine"

wears out.   Or, to take another metaphor, if you burn a candle with
a high flame, or at both ends, it will be brighter but it will also
burn down more quickly.   A certain amount of wear and tear is
unavoidable, otherwise the engine would stand still, the candle would
go out; in a word, you would be dead.   So the problem is not that
the body reacts with stress, but the degree of stress, i.e. the rate
of wear and tear, to which it is subject.   This varies from one
minute to another, depending partly on the body's properties and
partly on the external influences and demands, the stressors, to
which the body is exposed.   (A _stressor_ is thus something that
produces stress.)

Sometimes it is difficult to determine whether stress in a
particular situation is good or bad - to some extent this depends on
the standard one applies.   Take, for instance, the exhausted athlete
on the winner's stand or the newly appointed but stress-racked
executive.   Both have achieved their goals.   In terms of pure
accomplishment, one would have to say that the result was well worth
the effort.   In psychological terms, however, this is more doubtful
since a good deal of torment may have been needed to get so far -
long years of training or incessant overtime at the expense of family
life.   From the medical viewpoint they perhaps burnt their candle at
both ends.   The athlete may rupture a muscle or two, the executive
may develop an ulcer or a heart attack (Levi, 1967, 1968; Bronner
and Levi, 1973).

The stress of modern life

People often talk about "the stress of modern life".   But
stress has existed in all ages; neither are stress reactions confined
to man.   They occur throughout most of the animal kingdom and have
existed since the dawn of the human species.   They were around when
vertebrates emerged on earth 50 million years ago, and later when
mammals appeared; when four-footed creatures rose up on their hind
legs and began to acquire humanoid features about 3.5 million years
ago and, then 500,000 years ago, when the cerebral cortex grew to its
inordinate size and man became man.   Even then, fully recognisable
stress reactions existed but at that time they mostly served a
meaningful purpose, such as preparing the body for physical activity:
muscular work, or fight or flight, when danger loomed.   When our
uncivilised ancestors several hundred thousand years ago stood at the
mouth of their Stone-Age caves, with wild beasts closing in on them,

they responded to the danger. Various adaptive mechanisms in the body of the Stone-Age savage began to function automatically. His cerebral cortex would send a signal to the brain stem: danger, alarm, alert! His heart started beating more rapidly, his breathing accelerated, his muscles tensed. More adrenaline was released into the bloodstream and "fuel" was drawn from the sugar deposits in the liver and muscles. Likewise, more noradrenaline entered the bloodstream and drew fuel from the fat deposits. The additional fuel flowed to the muscles via the blood as our Stone-Age savage prepared himself for fight, flight and physical effort. Had he not so reacted, we would not be here today. The human species would have become extinct. Individuals without the capacity to react with stress fell by the wayside; but others who had this capacity survived, multiplied, and over millions of years populated the earth with a race, our own, that has a great capacity to react with stress (Levi, 1975b).

But in today's environments this mode of reacting tends to be impractical. We cannot fight our way out of financial difficulties or rely on our muscles to escape an unhappy event. Usually, we do nothing at all or we keep up appearances. Yet the smooth facade masks the selfsame stress reactions, now often to no reasonable purpose and possibly at the expense of the body, resulting in illness, especially if they are persistent or intensive or occur often (Levi, 1972).

What causes stress?

We can say that stress is caused by a misfit between our needs and capabilities and what our environment offers and demands. We need a certain amount of responsibility but the environment offers less or demands more. We need a certain amount of work but the environment offers either none at all (unemployment) or too much (Kagan and Levi, 1974). The same applies to "information". We can get too little information if, say, the management withholds important news about the future of some staff unit. Conversely, we can get too much information as when the flow of fact and figures is so great that we cannot pick out what really matters so that this sweeps by together with all the trivia.

Similarly, in the case of "change" it is no doubt true that never before have so many changes occurred so rapidly for so many as in our age. And change, even of the desired variety, can be excessive, leading to a feeling that "everything is in a state of flux". But there is also the opposite: a completely static society in which everything remains the same: no development, no growth, no change. Once again, a question of "too much or too little".

But the amount that is "too much" or "too little" is not the same for everyone, or even for the same individual in different situations. Sometimes we simply want to be left in peace. At other times, we want stimulation. What matters is the total situation not just a small segment.

Suppose we have had a terribly taxing day and come home exhausted. We are then unlikely to be particularly amused by our teen-age children listening to pop music at 100 decibels. We've already absorbed as much stimulation as we can tolerate and simply cannot take anymore. But then, having rested, on Sunday afternoon, perhaps we find the same loud, rhythmic 100 decibels more tolerable. The selfsame 100 decibels, for the selfsame person, but in a different mood. Stimulation piled upon stimulation: stimulation at work, in public, in family life and elsewhere. And when we are old, who knows, lying bed-ridden in a nursing home, waiting for a visit that doesn't happen, or in vain for the telephone to ring; our problem is still stress, but now from too little stimulation, not too much (Levi, 1984).

The poor fit between man and his environment also concerns our capacity and the environment's demands on this. Once again, the demands may be too high or too low. While we all have some capacity in various respects, there is an unfortunate tendency to reason that "if he can, so can I", or "I am just as good as the next person". Just as good, certainly, in the sense of equal worth as a human being, no one would dispute that. But not always just as good in the sense of being just as capable of performing, just as resistant, or just as tough, and this is where problems often arise. Our capacity does not always measure up to the demands placed on it. Others, or we ourselves, expect too much or too little of us or require the wrong things. In all such cases, we react with stress or, as the saying goes, "too much or too little spoils everything".

Demands can be too modest. Many women, for instance, have never had an opportunity to acquire an adequate education, that is, one equal to their abilities. An early marriage and children may have stood in the way. As a result, when they do venture into the world of work - with a low level of education and perhaps pushing 45 - they may have to put up with what they can get, even if the job demands far less than they can and want to achieve (Levi, 1978). They never get a real chance to show what they can do, a chance of harnessing the "horsepower" under their "hoods". The amount of work expected of them may be very great. This means that they are exposed to a combination of qualitative underdemand (a job that is too simple) and quantitative overdemand (too much to do). Stress is then the result.

Stress also arises out of another kind of misfit, namely, between our expectations and what we actually go through or experience. We all expect certain things of our jobs, our marriage, our children, or those with whom we work. For many of us, even quite reasonable expectations remain unsatisfied. In other instances it is our expectations that are unrealistic. Some people, for example, form ideas about marriage from weekly magazines or other literature which gives them a totally unrealistic notion of what awaits them.

Another cause of stress lies in role conflicts. We all have many roles, not just one. We are husbands or wives; we are our parents' children and our children's parents; we are brothers or sisters; friends; acquaintances; and we are bosses, comrades on the job and subordinates, all at the same time. We belong to different organisations. Conflicts can easily arise between several of these roles. The spirit of compromise entailed by our attempts to fill many roles also involves a stress-producing factor.

A common denominator of all these "misfits" is our lack of control over our situation. If we are in full control, we can adapt the environment to our abilities and needs, thereby restoring a good person-environment fit.

Differences in vulnerability and endurance

Besides being exposed to different kinds of strain, people differ in their vulnerability. An example may help to clarify this. The weight which an experienced long-shoreman has no difficulty in carrying on his back can produce serious pains in a receptionist or an office girl. The same conflict on the job may be shrugged off with a laugh by the mentally resilient, while those who are psychologically sensitive and touchy it can be the prelude to a nervous breakdown. So, as we see, the same situation can differ greatly in its stress-producing effect on different individuals and even on the

same individual at different times.   Further, different people are
variously equipped to cope with their life situation in general.
If a person is unhappy in his private life and then encounters major
problems at work, stress will be more serious then if the private
life was going well, even though the strain at work is exactly the
same (Levi, 1978, 1981a).

    We should also point out that human beings do not just passively
absorb the environment's impositions.   Moreover, both the environment
and our reactions to it can be controlled to some extent.   A person
can alter his environment or flee from his problems: he can appeal
for help or bury his head in the sand (Lazarus, 1966, 1976). He can cope
(cf. page 35).   Whatever his choice, it can influence his stress level.

Is stress necessarily harmful?

    In situations requiring muscular activity, stress reactions are
usually purposeful.   For a coalminer or stevedore, it serves to
release various "fuels" into the bloodstream and speed up the
circulation (the heart beats faster), breathing is accelerated so
that the blood picks up more oxygen, and the bloodstream, bearing
its "fuels", is directed to where it is most needed, namely the
muscles (Levi, 1971, 1972; Henry and Stephens, 1977; Elliott and
Eisdorfer, 1982).

    In the case of mental strain, a certain amount of stress can
give that little extra "boost" a person needs to give of his best,
whether in a talk, in negotiations, in trying to sell a product or
anything else.   But if this boost is too violent, the opposite
occurs: a block arises, our head becomes empty and we cannot think
of what we want to say.   As in any other situation, it is a question
of not too little, not too much, but just right.

    Strain in just the right dose is borne well by the body; it
stimulates the organism and may enhance its ability to perform and
make it tougher.   An athlete trains for a long time before running
the marathon.   A shy, inexperienced salesman waits until he has
warmed up a bit before tackling his most difficult customers.   Both
the athlete and the salesman mete out their strain in small doses.
Strain in just the right dose - one might even call it training -
can thus be something positive and stimulating and actually heighten
performance because it produces stress reactions which remain within
the body's ability to cope, exercising reasonable effort.   The
problem lies in arriving at what is "just right" for each individual.

It is not often that people are exposed to strains that are too moderate or too few. The opposite is far more common: strains which are too severe or taxing or which our bodies are too "old fashioned" to cope with.

As we have said, the body reacts to all sorts of stressors in accordance with, generally speaking, a single plan for defence. The endocrine glands and the autonomic nervous system (the part of the nervous system which cannot be controlled by the will), together constitute the body's most important means of defence. The Canadian scientist, Hans Selye, who introduced the term "stress", has coined a term for what happens in these two systems under strain: the general adaptation syndrome (Selye, 1971). The meaning of "adaptation" is clear, while "syndrome" implies that the different defence forces are co-ordinated.

The sequence of physiological events in the adaptation syndrome may be summed up as follows: the first and quickest reaction to stress comes from the autonomic nervous system whose two subsystems, the sympathetic and parasympathetic, together seek to bring about the necessary adjustments in bodily functions. The next step is an increased production of the stress hormone adrenaline from the adrenal medulla, in response to signals from the sympathetic nervous system. This stepped-up adrenaline production, together with signals from the hypothalamus (the anterior part of the brain stem), stimulates the pituitary to increase its hormone production. The pituitary hormones regulate the production of hormones by other endocrine glands, and these hormones in turn participate in various ways in the body's defence and adaptation reactions. The pituitary hormone most essential to this process is called ACTH and controls the adreno-cortical secretion of vital hormones - above all - cortisol.

In the case of mental strain, signals are sent from the cerebral cortex to the hypothalamus, from whence the autonomic nervous system is steered and the pituitary is influenced in the way described above.

How does stress feel?

We react to life's sundry stresses and strains. Our reactions may be described at three levels: subjective, behavioural and physiological.

Subjective experience

When we undergo strain - whether from excessive or insufficient demands, needs that have gone unmet, unfulfilled expectations, over-stimulation, understimulation, lack of personal control over one's situation, or role conflicts - most of us experience anxiety, uneasiness and dejection. Perhaps we even feel like a stranger to our existence. We question life's meaning.

In every organism, impulses flow continuously from the periphery to the higher nervous centres. These "proprioceptive impulses" constitute the "background noise" in most people and it is against this background of which we are seldom aware that reactions elicited by various stimuli from the environment or from changes in body functions are experienced. However, some people are prone to "suffer after-effects" and to interpret these impulses, in themselves quite normal (organ sensations), as symptoms of illness. Thus a person may experience pressure in the head, be tormented by "palpitations", feel tensions or "twitching" in the stomach or have difficulty in breathing, despite the fact that by all objective criteria the organ in question is structurally and functionally normal. In some cases, the troubles are experienced as so severe that the person has to go sick. The propensity to have such experiences may depend on the individual, but can also be linked to problems in the environment. It is conceivable, for instance, that understimulation at work (Levi, 1981a) or after retirement (Levi, 1984) allows this background noise to surge more readily to the surface of consciousness because there is no, or less, competition from signals from the current environment.

Some may say that these are in fact "simply" experiences, "simply" feelings, but this "simply" misses the point. If long periods of our life are marred by uneasiness and anxiety, or if the only life we shall ever have is spent in depression and the blues, that is serious enough in itself. On top of this, many people have such violent subjective reactions that they suffer, cease to function socially, seek medical assistance and stay away from work.

Behaviour

In addition (or instead), some of us begin to smoke 30 cigarettes a day and eventually may acquire a cancer of the lungs. Many seek consolation in alcohol and can develop liver damage. Some begin to take drugs; that is to say other drugs or more than the doctor has

prescribed.   Still others seek the extreme, the irreversible, self-
destructive way out: they try to take their life.   Three times as
many people in Sweden die at their own hands as in traffic.   It has
been calculated that every year about 2,000 people kill themselves
and about 20,000 try to do so (out of a population of 8.3 million).
And contrary to common belief, Sweden's suicide rates are in no way
among the highest in the world.   So these reactions can indeed be
crucial for health or illness, for life or death.   They are no less
important than the lead content in the air we breathe or the toxic
sewage in our rivers, lakes and streams; in both cases, our well-
being, our health and sometimes even our life, are at stake (Levi and
Andersson, 1975, 1979).

Physiological reactions

When a teacher faces his class, or a salesman an important
customer, the heart starts beating faster, breathing accelerates and
the muscles tense.   This is not just a feeling; it actually happens.
The adrenal glands produce more adrenaline, releasing fuel from the
sugar depots in the muscles and liver.   More noradrenaline is also
secreted, releasing fuel from fat depots (Levi, 1972; Elliott and
Eisdorfer, 1982; Weiss, Herd and Fox, 1981).

Usually, these stress reactions are mild and temporary and can
hardly be classified as symptoms of illness or even as precursors
of illness in the more restricted sense.   But since, in the long
run, they are often accompanied by discomfort (owing, for example,
to continuous and hence painful muscle tension, accelerated breathing,
which alters the body's carbon dioxide level, causing respiratory
alkalosis) or accelerated intestinal passage (leading to diarrhoea),
many people experience and describe them as an illness.   Moreover,
if they persist, the result can indeed be illness and disability.
Similarly, episodes of anxiety, unrest and depression can be labelled
"illness".   Such mental and/or physical symptoms are very
common and are a major cause of work absenteeism.   They are one of
many mechanisms which manifest the links between our psycho-social
environment and our health (Kagan and Levi, 1974; Vester, 1976;
Lohmann, 1978; Levi, 1979; Wolf, 1981).

If these or related reactions persist, if they are intense or
frequent, they may be presumed to place a strain on the organism and
cause damage not only to the functions but also to the structures of
our organs and organ systems.

A permanent state of alert

A few examples will illustrate this.   Suppose we are faced with unrealistic demands at work.   We have been called upon to reverse a product's falling sales and have been given little time in which to do so - in a situation, moreover, where the entire branch is beset by serious problems.   The days and months pass and, in spite of all our efforts, a series of earnings reports and forecasts forces us to acknowledge that the future is anything but bright.   We have taken on the impossible, yet persist in trying to attain it.

Not uncommonly, in such a situation, the heart starts beating faster, breathing accelerates, muscles tense and the stomach con-tracts.   More hydrochloric acid is produced in the stomach, blood pressure rises, the circulation speeds up - as if we were engaged in a physical fight or in physical flight.

Or suppose we are returning home from work and face the prospect of unpleasant scenes in our private life.   We expect arguments and recriminations or the bitter "silent treatment".   And that is how it is going to be next week, next month, next year, or maybe even ten years hence.   We see no way out.   We develop headaches or muscular pains.

Now let us consider this last symptom.   If a muscle is kept taut for a long time, it begins to hurt.   This is easily observed by holding a clenched fist for a quarter of an hour or so; pain begins to set in and gradually becomes quite severe.

Now no one would adopt such practices consciously and deliber-ately.   But unintentionally and unconsciously we may tense the muscles, say, on top of our head, which are used to furrow the brow, or our chest muscles.   If we do this hard and long, it begins to hurt.   But usually a patient thinks, not in terms of muscles, but about parts of the body.   Once we begin to think in this way, the after-effect grows and we become more and more uneasy.   The symptoms intensify the worries, which intensify the symptoms, which intensify the worries, and so on.

From our everyday experience we know that various emotions, such as anger, hate, anxiety and sorrow, are normally accompanied by quite significant functional changes in the organism.   However, usually we soon manage to find an outlet for pent up feelings - we scream at the person we are angry with, get over our sorrow by obtaining solace, by crying, etc. - but this is not always possible.   Unlike most of us, some people have difficulty in living out and expressing their feelings. In other cases, pressure from the environment - society, the family, workplace, etc. - may be so great and so enduring that not even a mentally strong person can cope with the situation; that is, change or accept it. Finally, there are others who experience even minor everyday reversals as grave misfortunes and react accordingly.

In some such cases, emotions like anger or anxiety linger on instead of passing over. When this happens, the accompanying changes in bodily functions also persist and produce symptoms in some of the ways described above.

Wear and tear damages cells

A high stress level means a high rate of wear and tear in the body, which in turn augments ill health and infirmity. The type of ill health and infirmity it produces will, however, depend in part on genetic factors, and in part on the effects left by earlier influences from the environment (e.g. earlier illnesses). Hence it is thought that the same strain will cause ulcers in one person, high blood pressure in another, and perhaps a heart attack in a third, but leaving a fourth one in good health.

This does not mean that psychological factors are important or even exclusive causes in all forms of illnesses, such as ulcers, high blood pressure, toxic goitre or asthma. Such illnesses come in many guises. But in some it is possible, perhaps even probable, that psychological factors are the primary or contributing cause of illness, which is then usually described as psychosomatic. In other cases, the role of psychological factors is doubtless more modest.

It may be relevant here to refer briefly to some recent research which has shed light on this interplay between psychological and physical factors. For reasons of space, the account is confined to ulcers, high blood pressure and myocardial infarction.

Ulcers

The proportion of persons who get an ulcer at some time during their lives is as high as 10 to 12 per cent. Every year ulcers and related disorders account for many millions of days lost through sickness. The probable relation between certain forms of this disease and mental strain has been demonstrated convincingly in what

is now a classical experiment, conducted with the man, Tom, by
Harold G. Wolff and Stewart Wolf, two American professors. Tom,
who worked in their research laboratory as a janitor, had a stomach
fistula, a "window" in the abdominal wall adjacent to the stomach.
The fistula had been made necessary by an injury to the oesophagus
when Tom was a child (Wolf, 1971; Wolf et al., 1979).

Like all other employees, Tom had to cope with his share of the
stresses and strains of everyday working life. However, in Tom's
case, some of his stress reactions could be readily observed by
keeping a close eye on the stomach mucosa through the window in his
abdominal wall. After each complaint levied at Tom, it was noted
that the stomach muscles contracted, as in a convulsion, the stomach
stepped up its production of hydrocholoric acid and the gastric
mucosa reddened especially when Tom felt angry or irritated. There
is evidence that it is, indeed, just functional changes of this sort
which lie behind the development of certain kinds of ulcer. In
animal experiments, ulcers have been induced by exposing animals to
various stressors. Thus bleeding wounds have appeared in the
stomach mucosa of rats prevented from moving about, in monkeys
continually forced to make decisions and in a number of other animal
species forced to live together under crowded conditions. We should
point out, however, that these ulcers differ in certain respects from
those found in humans (Wolf et al., 1979).

High blood pressure

Another very widespread disease in which stress may play a role
is "high blood pressure" (Brod, 1971; Weiner, 1979; Obrist, 1981;
Weiss, Herd and Fox, 1981; Svensson, 1983). During the Finnish
winter war (1939-40) and during the Second World War, many front-line
soldiers who had always enjoyed good health suddenly displayed a
rather considerable rise in blood pressure, which receded only slowly
after they had been sent home from the front.

Work stress on the job is likewise thought to contribute to high
blood pressure. Series of studies have shown that high blood
pressure is especially common among telephone exchange operators and
teachers (Rozwadowska-Dowzenko, Kotlarska and Zawadskj, 1956;
Mjasnikov, 1961). A persistent hypertension has been induced
experimentally in rats exposed to continuing loud noise and in cats
held in cages surrounded by yelping dogs.

In many cultures (but by no means all), blood pressure increases with age.   Physiologist James Henry and epidemiologist J. Cassel sum up today's knowledge about this correlation in the following words:

> A man living in a stable society and well equipped by his cultural background to deal with the familiar world around him will not show a rise in blood pressure with age.   This thesis holds whether he is a modern technocrat who became a fighter pilot early in life or a Stone-Age bushman who is a skilled hunter-gatherer living in the Kalahari Desert.   However, when radical cultural changes disrupt his familiar environment with a new set of demands for which past acculturation has left him unprepared, his social assets are then critical.   Should they fail to protect him, he will be exposed to emotional upheavals and ensuing neuro-endocrine disturbances that may eventuate in cardiovascular disease (Henry and Stephens, 1977).

Myocardial infarction

Studies carried out in the United States have shown that strongly aggressive, competitive, career-driven - Type A - persons who concentrate on scrambling up the social ladder of success at any price in a relentless race against time have a higher lipid content in the blood, quicker blood clotting time, a higher excretion of stress hormones with the urine and a higher risk of contracting coronary disease later in life than persons with a quieter, more casual and "more easy-going" life-style (Henry and Stephens, 1977). The positive correlation between the latter life-style and a low risk of coronary disease has been confirmed in other studies. Stewart Wolf, for example, found that descendants of Italian immi-grants who came to Roseto, Pennsylvania (United States), around the turn of the century, differed from the population in neighbouring communities in three respects.   They lived quieter, happier and more contented life; they had a considerably lower lipid content in their blood even though they ate at least as much fat as their neighbours; and their mortality rate from heart attacks was less than half that in the neighbouring, more competitive communities and, moreover, less than half the national average (cf. also Wolf, 1981; Obrist, 1981; Denolin, 1982: Elliott and Eisdorfer, 1982).

In several series of Swedish studies (Levi, Frankenhaeuser and Gardell, 1982) it has been shown that the output of noradrenaline and adrenaline (the "stress hormones" of the sympathetic nervous system and the adrenal medulla) is stepped up in almost every form of exposure to psychosocial stressors.   It is the job of these hormones to put the body in a state of alert, to prepare it for fight or

flight.   As part of this preparation, free fatty acids - the fuel
for the body's energy-consuming processes - are released from the
body's fat depots (cf. Levi, 1971, 1972; Henry and Stephens, 1977).
Thus, when a person is uneasy or tense, the fat content in the blood
increases.   (Such a rise has been observed in accountants during
the month just before the end of their firm's accounting year.)
However, the fight or flight for which our body prepares us seldom
occurs today.   We have learned to suppress such impulses in our
actions.   But changes in body chemistry cannot be suppressed.
According to studies by Raab (1971), a persistently increased
production of these stress hormones and of cortisol is likely to be
detrimental to various organs, including the heart.   It is possible
that the excess, unconsumed lipids in the blood, are gradually
deposited in the vessel walls which, in turn, is thought to cause
hardening of the arteries. Quite probably, another four factors
actively contribute to such conditions (cf. Hamburg, Nightingale and
Kalmar, 1979; US Surgeon General, 1979).   The first is that we eat
too much in general and too much fat in particular.   The second is
the sedentary life most of us lead.   The third and fourth are that
we are smoking more and drinking more alcohol.   Animal experiments
have also been used to induce heart disease.   Soviet scientists
were able to induce changes, ultimately fatal, in the heart tissue
of the leader of a baboon pack simply by "dethroning" him (Lapin and
Cherkovich, 1971).

STRESS IN INDUSTRY

2

Physical and psychosocial stressors

Discussions of occupational stress often tend to omit <u>physical</u> environmental factors in spite of the fact that such factors can influence the worker not only physically and chemically (e.g. direct effects on the brain by organic solvents) but also psychosocially. The latter effects can be secondary to the distress caused by, say, odours, glare, noise, extremes with regard to air temperature and humidity, etc. They can also be due to the worker's <u>awareness</u>, <u>suspicion</u> or <u>fear</u> that he is exposed to life-threatening chemical hazards or to accident risks. Thus organic solvents, for instance, can influence the human brain directly, whatever the worker's awareness, feelings and beliefs. They can also influence him more indirectly, secondary to the unpleasantness of their smell. Thirdly, they can affect him because he may know of or suspect that the exposure may be harmful to him (Levi, 1981b).

Real life conditions usually imply a combination of many exposures. These might become superimposed on each other in an additive way (1+1=2) or synergistically (1+1=3). The straw which breaks the camel's back may therefore be a rather trivial environmental exposure but one that comes on top of a very considerably existing environmental load. Unfortunately, very little is known of the net effects of such combined exposures (cf. Kahn, 1981; Wolf, Bruhn and Goodell, 1978; Cooper and Payne, 1980; Shostak, 1979; Warshaw, 1979: Moss, 1981: MacKay and Cox, 1979).

With regard to <u>psychosocial</u> stressors in the work environment, evidence exists (Blohmke and Reimer, 1980) to support the assumption that a number of properties of systems design and job content are critical not only with regard to job satisfaction but also for health (Levi, 1972, 1981a; Frankenhaeuser, 1976, 1981; Frankenhaeuser and Johansson, 1976; Frankenhaeuser and Gardell, 1976; Johansson et al., 1978; Gardell, 1979, 1980; Levi, Frankenhaeuser and Gardell, 1982):

(a) Quantitative overload, i.e. too much to do, time pressure, repetitive work flow in combination with one-sided job demands and superficial attention. This is to a great extent the typical feature of mass production technology and routinised office work.

(b) Qualitative underload, i.e. too narrow and one-sided job content, lack of stimulus variation, no demands on creativity or problem-solving, or low opportunities for social interaction. These jobs seem to become more common with automation and the increased use of computers in both offices and manufacturing, even though there may be instances of the opposite.

(c) Lack of control over one's situation, especially in relation to work pace and working methods.

(d) Lack of social support from fellow workers and at home (House, 1981).

Very often, several of these characteristics appear together and have a joint effect on health and well-being. A representative sample of the male Swedish labour force has been examined with respect to symptoms of depression, excessive fatigue, cardio-vascular disease and mortality. The workers whose jobs were characterised by heavy loads, together with low control over the work situation, were represented disproportionately on all these symptom variables. The least probability for illness and death was found among groups with moderate loads combined with high control over the work situation (Ahlbom, Karasek and Theorell, 1977; Karasek, 1979, 1981). Briefly, then, evidence exists that work stress may be problematic in two different ways. First, there may be a direct relation between certain objective conditions at work, physiological and psychological stress and ill health. Second, certain stress conditions may create fatigue and/or passivity in individuals and thus make it more difficult for them to involve themselves actively in changing those working conditions - including physical and chemical risk factors - that may be detrimental to health. This latter aspect is especially relevent when interest focuses on ill-health prevention on the systems level (McLean, Black and Colligan, 1977).

As pointed out by Gardell (1976), Wilensky (1981) and others, the ill effects of mass production technology include the alienation of the worker not just during working hours but with a spill-over to leisure time. An increase in apathy may grow out of this dis-affection, resulting in a decreased willingness of the worker to take part in activities outside work.

From a psychophysiological viewpoint, it seems reasonable that the speed with which a person "unwinds" after work will influence the total wear on his or her biological system. Hence, the speed of unwinding is also likely to influence the extent to which stress at work is carried over into leisure time (Frankenhaeuser, 1977a, b).

There are large inter-individual differences in the temporal pattern of psychophysiological and psychoendocrine stress responses. Experimental results indicate (e.g. Johansson and Frankenhaeuser, 1973) that "rapid adrenaline decreasers" tend to be psychologically better balanced and more efficient in achievement situations than "slow adrenaline decreasers". An equally important finding is that the time for unwinding varies predictably with the individual's state of general well-being. Thus, in a group of industrial workers, the proportion of "rapid adrenaline decreases" was significantly higher after than before a vacation period, which had improved the workers' physical and psychological well-being (Johansson, 1976).

Another example of conditions associated with slow unwinding was provided in a recent study (Rissler, 1977) of stress and coping patterns of female clerks in an insurance company. It was hypoth-esised that the additional overtime load would call for increases in adaptive efforts, the effects of which would not be confined to the extra work-hours, but would also materialise during and after regular work-days. The results supported this hypothesis, in that catecholamine excretion was significantly increased throughout the overtime period, both during the day and in the evening. As hypothesised, there was further a pronounced elevation of adrenaline output in the evenings, although these had been spent under non-work conditions at home (Frankenhaeuser, 1979, 1981). This was accompanied by a markedly elevated heart rate as well as feelings of irritability and fatigue. In sum, these results demonstrate how the effects of work overload may spread to leisure hours.

Impact of mass production technology

Over the past century, work has been _fragmented_, changing from the completion of a well-defined job activity, with a distinct and recognised end-product, into one of numerous, narrow and highly specified sub-units with little apparent relation to the end-product. The growing size of factory units has tended to result in a long chain of command between management and the individual worker, accentuating remoteness between the two groups. The worker becomes remote also from the consumer, since rapid elaborations for marketing, distribution and selling interpose many steps between producer and consumer (Maule et al., 1973).

Mass production normally involves not just a pronounced fragmentation of the work process but also a _decrease in worker control_ of this, partly because work organisation, work content and pace are determined by the machine system, partly as a result of the detailed pre-planning that is necessary in such systems. All this usually results in monotony, social isolation, lack of freedom and time pressure, with possible long-term effects on health and well-being. Mass production, moreover, favours the introduction of piece-rate systems. In addition, heavy investment in machinery, alone or combined with shorter hours of work, has increased the proportion of people working in shifts. Another effect of the emphasis on mass production, and eventually on automation, is that large industrial concerns have grown at the expense of medium and small enterprises.

Work on the _assembly line_, organised on the principle of the "moving belt", is characterised by the machine system's rigorous control over the worker. The job is understimulating in the sense that individual operations often are extremely simple, there are no options for variety in either pace or content, and the opportunities for social interaction are often minimal. At the same time the work contains elements of overload, such as _rapid pacing_, coercion and demands for sustained attention. The worker has no control over pace and his body posture and motility are narrowly restricted (Dolan and Arsenault, 1980).

In their now classic study, Walker and Guest (1952) showed how assembly-line work, with its mechanical element and rigidly fragmented tasks, was accompanied by discontent, stress and alienation among the workers. Similar results have been reported by several investigators (e.g. Blauner, 1964; Zdravomyslov and Yadov, 1966). Studies that focus on the task structure and its variations within similar technologies underscore that the restrictions imposed on the workers as to exercising skill and control affect not only alienation but also mental health (Kornhauser, 1965; Gardell, 1971).

By integrating concepts and methods from psychophysiology and social psychology, it has been possible to link both job dissatisfaction and physiological stress responses to specific job characteristics (Frankenhaeuser, 1980a, 1981).

In a study of sawmill workers (Frankenhaeuser and Gardell, 1976) interest focused on a group classified as high-risk workers on the basis of the extremely constricted nature of their job. The psychoneuroendocrine stress responses of this group were compared with those of a control group of workers from the same mill, whose job was not as constricted physically or mentally. The results showed that catecholamine (adrenaline and noradrenaline) excretion during work was significantly higher in the high-risk group than in the controls. Furthermore, the time course was strikingly different in the two groups, catecholamine excretion decreasing towards the end of the workday in the control group, but increasing in the high-risk group. Interview data showed that inability to relax after work was a serious complaint in the latter group. Moreover, absenteeism and frequency of psychosomatic symptoms were very high in this group. The data suggest that the high stress level in the acute work situation and the symptoms of failing health had a common origin in the repetitive, coercive nature of the job. Thus, correlation analysis showed consistent relations between psychoneuroendocrine stress response patterns and job characteristics in terms of monotony, constraint and lack of personal control (Johansson, Aronsson and Lindström, 1978). These relationships were examined further by comparing subgroups of workers who differed with regard to specific job characteristics as rated by experts. The results indicated that stress, as reflected in catecholamine excretion, was highest when the job was highly repetitive, when the worker had to maintain the same posture throughout working hours, and when the work pace was controlled by the machine system. Thus lack of control again stands out as the critical factor. The modifying influence of controllability on psychoneuroendocrine stress responses has also been demonstrated in laboratory studies of human subjects by Frankenhaeuser and her collaborators (e.g. Frankenhaeuser and Rissler, 1970; Lundberg and Frankenhaeuser, 1978, 1980; Frankenhaeuser, Lundberg and Forsman, 1980).

Piece-rate systems

A related issue is the relation between stress and a remuneration system involving some type of piece-rate work (see review by Levi, 1972; Gardell, 1979).   The common factor in piece-rate systems is the payment of a price or rate per piece or unit òf work; this price may be uniform at all levels of output or may vary as production rises (ILO, 1951).

Systems by which workers' earnings increase more than output are based on the philosophy that the workers should benefit from the reduction of overhead costs that is achieved as output rises.   Under the high piece-rate system,workers' earnings do not relate linearly to output, as they do under straight piece work; instead, the increment grows with each increase in output.   For example, the hourly increment to pay may be 1.33 per cent for each 1 per cent increase in output.

Accelerating premium systems are based on the principle that earning increments are small for low and average levels of output, but become increasingly larger as output exceeds the average.   The increments may thus differ for éach 1 per cent increase in output. At low output the differences are small and scarcely apparent to the worker, but at high output they provide a powerful stimulus to the worker to step up his output more and more.

It is generally agreed that piece rates strengthen motivation at work and are thereby one of the most important incentives to boost productivity.   It is often claimed that they are a necessary prerequisite of good performance, yielding higher earnings for workers and lower costs for management (Levi, 1972).   Yet little is known about the psychological and physiological effects of this remuneration system.   It is, for example, conceivable that excessively strong motivation on a regular basis could lead to undue strain, which might be harmful to health and well-being.   The desire - or necessity - to earn more can, for a time, induce the individual to work harder than is good for the organism and to ignore mental and physical "warnings", such as a feeling of tiredness, nervous troubles and functional disturbances in various organs or organ systems.   Another possible effect is that the employee, bent on raising his output and earnings, infringes safety regulations, thereby increasing the risk of occupational disease and of accidents to himself and others (e.g. lorry drivers on piece rates) (Levi, 1976).   Again, older or handicapped persons working in groups with collective piece rates are liable to come under social pressure from their fellow workers, and workers with individual piece rates may conceivably be less disposed to help each other.

In discussing the existing scientific evidence of non-economic effects of piece rates and the results of practical experiments with wage payment methods, it should be observed that one is dealing with a complex reality, which makes it very hard to isolate the effects of piece work from other factors which simultaneously affect the individual's feelings and behaviour. To take one example, work content and the remuneration system are closely inter-related. More or less by definition, the piece-rated jobs are those with operations that lend themselves to measurement. As a rule, this also means a rather narrow and repetitive job.

In a large state-owned mining company, the introduction of fixed salaries was evaluated by an independent research team (one-year follow up) as well as by the company itself (three-year follow up). Both studies showed a steep decline in severe accidents (cases requiring more than 90 days sick leave), a smaller decline in medium severe cases (7-90 days of sick leave) and a rise in minor accidents. Both studies conclude that fixed wages signified less stress and less risk-taking. In the independent study the rise in minor accidents was explained by the possibilities for workers under fixed wages to attend to minor accidents without loss of income. The company study also reported an overall loss in productivity by 10 per cent in the mining operation and no decline in productivity in the more automated dressing plants (Kronlund, 1974; Kjellgren, 1975).

In Swedish forest industries, one-year follow-up studies of the introduction of fixed wages in logging show a reduction in severe accidents. In one case, the total number of accidents decreased by 10 per cent while days lost through accidents were reduced by 50 per cent (Swedish Forest Service, 1975). Both companies report productivity losses of about 10 to 15 per cent but at the same time increased product quality (SCA-tidningen, 26 Nov. 1975).

The above observations from epidemiological studies are supported by experimental investigations (Levi, 1964, 1972). Healthy female office clerks were studied under conditions very similar to those involved in their everyday work. Highly progressive piece rates were introduced on the first and third day of the study and were found to result in significant increases in productivity but also in feelings of rush, fatigue and physical discomfort, in adrenaline and noradrenaline excretion and in urine flow.

In summary, these and related findings point to piece-rate work
being a factor with several negative aspects from the viewpoint of
stress, health, well-being and safety.   Above all, piece-rate
systems seem to induce an intensified working rhythm, a strong
taking of risks and competition between individuals or teams
(Pöyhönen, 1975).   Obviously, they may also lead to increased
productivity, but possibly at a cost carried by the worker and
society at large.

Highly automated work processes

An important question is whether occupational health and well-
being will be improved, while the strain on the workers diminishes,
by a transition to automated production systems where the repetitive,
manual elements are taken over by machines, and the workers are left
with mainly supervisory controlling functions.   This kind of work
is generally rather skilled, it is not regulated in detail, and the
worker is free to move about (Blauner, 1964;   Gardell, 1971).
Accordingly, the introduction of automation is generally considered
to be a positive step, partly because it eliminates many of the dis-
advantages of the mass production technique.   However, this holds
true mainly for those stages of automation where the operator is
indeed assisted by the computer and maintains some control over its
services.   If, however, operator skills and knowledge are gradually
taken over by the computer - a possible development if decision-
making is left to economists and technologists - a new impoverish-
ment of work may result, with the reintroduction of monotony, social
isolation and lack of control.   Only when the computer is introduced
as an advanced tool to assist and help the worker will the outcome be
beneficial.   With the striving toward maximum automation, man may
again become - the tool of his own tools!

For these reasons, the work conditions of control-room operators
in large-scale plants deserve special attention (Bainbridge,
1978;   Johansson and Gardell, 1978;   Frankenhaeuser, 1981).
Monitoring a process calls for acute attention and readiness to act
throughout a monotonous term of duty, a requirement that does not
match the brain's need for a moderately varied flow of stimuli in
order to maintain optimal alertness.   It is well documented that
the ability to detect critical signals declines rapidly even during
the first half-hour in a monotonous environment (e.g. Broadbent,
1971).   In addition, the fact that the process operators work in

shifts means that they may have to perform their attention-demanding
task also when "out of phase" with their biological rhythm, i.e. when
adrenaline secretion is low and ability to concentrate is reduced
(Levi, 1972; Fröberg, Karlsson, Levi and Lidberg, 1975a, b).   To
this must be added the strain inherent in the awareness that temporary
inattention and even an intrinsically slight error could have exten-
sive economic and other disastrous consequences (Frankenhaeuser,
1977c, 1981; Levi, 1981a, b).   These are the demands imposed on,
for example, the process operator in the control room of nuclear
power plants (Frankenhaeuser, 1980b).

Other critical aspects of process control are associated with
very special demands on mental skill.   The operators are concerned
with symbols - abstract signals on instrument arrays - and are not
in touch with the actual product of their work.   Research is needed
to analyse the psychological implications of such requirements.

High technical skill is required of process operators, yet they
spend most of their time in monotonous monitoring.   How, in the long
run, will these highly skilled operators cope with conditions that
utilise their skill during only a fraction of their work hours?

While we have referred mainly to industrial automation, similar
questions arise in connection with highly computerised administrative
work.   Office workers may spend up to 90 per cent of their day at a
computer terminal.   As long as the computer system functions
adequately, the work runs very smoothly.   But the moment the
computer breaks down, the worker is helpless and forced to remain
in a state of passive expectation for an unpredictable period of
time, turned into a "bottle-neck", holding up the flow of work
(Frankenhaeuser, 1981).   These mechanical breakdowns occur irregularly but tend to be frequent and always unpredictable.   They
constitute a source of stress, reflected at both the psychological
and the physiological levels (Johansson, 1979; Johansson and
Aronsson, 1980).   Here, as in the case of highly automated
industrial production systems, stress research is needed to provide
knowledge that can aid in guiding technological developments to suit
human needs and abilities.   The aim should be to achieve a level of
automation that is optimal for ascertaining a meaningful work content
and makes adequate demands on workers' skills.   Optimum automation,
thus defined, is not likely to be the same as maximum readily available automation.

Impact of shift work

Cyclic changes over a period of time are a property of all
organic life and as such of great evolutionary importance.   A
special example of this rhythmicity is the circadian (circa dies
(Lat.) = about 24 hours) rhythm.   Generally, circadian rhythms have
their maxima during the active part of the 24 hours and minima during
the inactive part.   A multitude of physiological and psychological
functions have been shown to exhibit circadian rhythms.   From the
dawn of mankind's history until quite recently, these circadian
rhythms have been beautifully adapted to the environmental demands
on man, favouring a variety of life and species-preserving activities
during the day and sleep during the night so that "batteries are re-
charged" (Akerstedt and Levi, 1978;   Levi, 1981b;   cf. also Maurice,
1975).

As mentioned above, the increasing demand for services and the
introduction of extremely expensive and complex modern technology
have created social structures which require greater human occupational activity around the clock.   Such circumstances have led to
some individuals being assigned work in shifts around the clock.
However, in the case of shift work, these rhythmical biological
changes do not necessarily coincide with corresponding environmental
demands.   Here, the organism may "step on the gas" and activation
occur at a time when the worker has to sleep (during the day after
a night shift) and deactivation correspondingly occurs at night when
he is often expected to work and be alert.   A further complication
arises because he usually lives in a social environment that is not
designed for the needs of shiftworkers.   Last, but not least, he
must adapt to regular or irregular changes in environmental demands,
as in the case of rotating shifts.

Work in two shifts creates fewer problems, apart from those of
an early start for the morning shift, which usually begins at 6 a.m.
(access to breakfast?   transportation?), and the effects of the
afternoon shift on interaction with pre-school and schoolchildren,
relatives and friends and participation in cultural, political and
union activities (Magnusson and Nilsson, 1979).   In the case of the
continuous three-shift work rhythm, on the other hand, disturbances
seem to be unavoidable.   The important thing here is to secure a
relatively long continuous free time after a relatively short night
shift to minimise and make up for a sleep deficit.   The most negative
of all work schedules are irregular shifts, which often occur in

transportation services, for example. Here, adaptational demands
become part of ordinary life, with no predictability and few possibilities for coping. In addition, not only sleeping times but
sleeping quarters too are changed irregularly and tend to be inadequate.

The temporal demands made on the shiftworker by his work
schedules are well known. Less is known of the ability of the
individual to match these demands and of the psychobiological "costs"
of such adaptation.

Some of these problems have been studied at the Laboratory for
Clinical Stress Research in a series of investigations utilising
interdisciplinary experimental as well as epidemiological approaches
(Akerstedt, 1976; Akerstedt and Fröberg, 1976).

Laboratory experiments. In the first series of studies,
attempts were made to identify the properties of the endogenous
temporal variation of some important physiological and psychological
functions, i.e. to study circadian biological rhythms in the absence
of the normal time cues. To this end, more than 100 normal, healthy
volunteers of both sexes were exposed to three days and three nights
of continuous work (Levi, 1972). In spite of the strict standard-
isation and equalisation of environmental stimuli over the entire
period, most circadian rhythms persisted throughout the vigil, with
pronounced decreases in adrenaline excretion and body temperature,
shortfalls in performance and increases in fatigue ratings and
melatonin excretion taking place in the small hours (Levi, 1972;
Fröberg et al., 1975a, b; Fröberg, 1977; Akerstedt and Fröberg, 1977).

Interdisciplinary observational studies. A logical second
step was to apply this information of persistent circadian rhythms
to a real-life situation, where environmental demands conflicted
with such rhythms. In this study, physiological, psychological,
chronobiological and social reactions were investigated in response
to the introduction of three weeks of night work in habitual daytime
workers. It was found that although the endocrine system does
indeed start to adapt to the environmental demands induced by shift
work - by "stepping on the gas" to keep awake at night and "slowing
down" in the day to allow for some sleep - the usual one-week cycle
does not suffice for a complete adaptation to the transformation of
night into day and vice versa. Not even three weeks of night work
are enough to cause an inversion of the circadian rhythms in all
subjects - in most, the original circadian rhythms either flatten
out or persist, causing fatigue, difficulties in sleeping and

possible indigestion.   In addition, switching from habitual daywork
to three weeks of night work is accompanied by increases in a number
of indices of physiological stress and in social problems in both
the workers and their families (Theorell and Akerstedt, 1976;
Akerstedt and Theorell, 1976).

To confirm the observation above, the next step was to study
the well-being of larger groups of shiftworkers also in an epidemiological manner.   To this end, several hundred shiftworkers were
studied with health questionnaire techniques under conditions where
self-selection - or movement away from - shift work was minimal
(i.e. no other jobs available in the area of residence).   The
results showed higher frequencies of sleep, mood, digestive and
social disturbances among the shiftworkers than among the day
workers.   The complaints about well-being reached their peak during
the night shift (Akerstedt and Torsvall, 1977a, b).

Real-life experiments.   Also, while in a natural experiment
one group was retained on continuous three-shift work, a comparable
experimental group was switched to two-shift work and another to day
work, everything else being held constant and equal.   In a two-year
follow up it was demonstrated that the change to work schedules
without night shift brought with it an improvement in physical,
mental and social well-being (Akerstedt and Torsvall, 1978).   In
contrast, the control group which remained on its habitual three-
shift work schedule did not improve in well-being.

Another experimental study was conducted on police officers
habitually working in rapidly rotating shifts (counter-clockwise) in
the Greater Stockholm region.   What was assumed to be an improved
work shedule (clockwise rotation instead of counter-clockwise) was
prepared, introduced and evaluated in an intensive, interdisciplinary
cross-over study and found to result in increase in well-being and
decrease in stress measures generally considered to be risk factors
for coronary heart disease, namely serum triglycerides, uric acid and
glucose (Orth-Gomér and Olivegard Landén, 1981).

This, then, illustrates that shift work does indeed cause
reduced well-being for most of those concerned,due to the misfit
between demands of work-hour placement and the temporal, physiological, psychological and social patterns of the individual.

These kinds of studies have not only a theoretical but potentially also a practical significance.   The second study (three
weeks of night work) did not prove conclusively that night work was

harmful to all subjects but it gave sufficient evidence of risk and
dissatisfaction for both management and workers to consider it to be
undesirable under the circumstances.   The risk was thought to be
not worth the modest advantages so the National Swedish Railway
Company agreed to eliminate night work for this specific group of
railway workers.

In summary, these studies and a critical review of the scientific literature justify the following conclusions (Akerstedt et al.,
1978; Akerstedt, 1979).   Physical, mental and social problems and
complaints increase with the introduction of night shifts and
decrease if night shifts are eliminated.   In workers on rotating
three-shift patterns, complaints are usually most pronounced during
the night shift.   Major concerns are sleep and digestion problems.
There is no adaptation to shift work with increasing length of
exposure.   Although there is no overall increase in absenteeism in
shiftworkers compared to day workers, increased absenteeism is found
in elderly shiftworkers.   Problems of health and well-being and
social problems tend to coincide in the same individuals.   Workers
on permanent night shift exhibit a better biological adaptation than
those on rotating shifts, in the sense that they exhibit a reversal
of the circadian rhythm seen in day workers, i.e. their organism
"steps on the gas" during night hours and slows down correspondingly
during day hours, allowing adequate performance levels during the
night and sleep during the day.   So, although some information has
been generated, more knowledge is needed on who is at risk, under
what circumstances and through which mechanisms.

Noise and vibration

Modern technical machinery has considerably decreased the
physical burden of work.   An unfavourable side-effect of this
largely favourable development has been the creation of noise and
vibration.   Noise hampers the intelligibility of speech and masks
acoustical signals.   It disturbs attention and concentration.   The
importance of noise as an irritation and disturbance in working life
has been amply documented.   A great deal is also known concerning
the harmful effects of noise on hearing (see ILO, 1977a).

A majority of industrial workers today are probably exposed to
industrial noise of a potentially damaging quality and intensity.
It is well known that in most of them, this leads to a successive
decrease in hearing ability.   Far less is known, on the other hand,

about the connection between work noise and physical and mental
health (apart from the hearing function).

It seems likely that, in the dawn of history, noise often served
as a signal of danger or was otherwise a characteristic of a situation
requiring muscular work.   In order to cope optimally with a challeng-
ing or hostile situation or even to survive, the human organism
responded to noise by a preparation for action, inter alia, by a
non-specific adaptive reaction pattern, namely stress.

It does so still.   A very large number of studies have clearly
documented the influence of noise on various nervous and hormonal
functions.   Reactions in these functions lead in turn to secondary
reactions in a large number of organs and organ systems.

The connection between noise and disease is considerably less
certain.   It is true that in animal experiments noise has been
proved capable of producing more or less permanent disruptions of
various bodily functions.   But the noise levels in these studies
have often been extremely high, besides which the sensitivity of
various animal species to noise differs appreciably from that of man.
Epidemiological studies provide some support for pathological effects.
Cohen (1973) compared sickness absence during five years in two
groups of 500 workers each.   One group worked in very noisy and
the other in less noisy surroundings.   The workers exposed to noise
displayed a higher general incidence of ill health, a higher rate of
sickness absence and a higher accident rate.   Their medical problems
included muscular symptoms and disruptions of the cardiac, circulatory
and digestive systems.   Several other studies report a greater incidence of high blood pressure among workers exposed to noise, as well
as of functional cardiac complaints and of gastric ulcers (Levi,
1981b).   There further appears to be a positive connection between
exposure to noise and neurotic complaints and social conflicts.

All these findings, however, have to be interpreted with
caution.   Working environments with high noise levels may have
other negative characteristics too and various selection phenomena
may be at work among these groups of employees, just as in other
cases.

Closely related to noise is vibration.   This is caused by
various impact, rotary and impact rotary tools.   Many of these
cause local vibration, including choppers, hammer drills, pneumatic
and riveting hammers, ramming machines and many others (Polezhayev
et al., 1974).   In mechanised transportation and in several

industries, workers are exposed to <u>generalised</u> vibration.   Here,
not only the vibrating object but also the body and its organs are
displaced in various planes, horizontally, vertically or at any
angle.   Both types of vibration clearly have unfavourable effects.
They involve a considerable expenditure of nervous energy and cause
fatigue.   Extreme exposure may even lead to disorders of the nervous
and vascular systems and of internal organ activity.

Machinery and tools

There are two kinds of muscular activity: dynamic (rhythmic
work) and static (postural work).   The latter rapidly leads to
painful fatigue and is a waste of energy.   In spite of this well-
known fact (Grandjean, 1969), countless workers work in one or more
of the following situations:

(a) in stooping or unnatural body positions, flexing the trunk or
     the head;

(b) with the arms constantly extended, either forwards or sideways;

(c) in a standing position, where sitting would be preferable;

(d) with sub-optimal height of the working area, making it difficult
     for them to see clearly what they do and to keep a comfortable
     body posture;

(e) with hand grips, levers, tools and other equipment which are
     difficult to clasp, locate or move, particularly in simultaneous
     operations;

(f) with display instruments (pointers, dials, counters) that are
     difficult to read with regard to absolute values and changes.

All this contributes strongly to the stress of working life,
acts as a threat to health and well-being and decreases productivity.

Buildings and premises

It has been claimed that buildings act as a third skin (the
second being clothing), a selectively permeable interface between
organism and environment, affecting and being affected by both.
Buildings also have social functions.   They permit, encourage or
even impose the congregation of people and their interaction, or at
least their sharing of the same experiences.   Their cellular
structure may also be used to maintain boundaries between persons
(Abercrombie, 1976).

Buildings also have a symbolic value. Churches, government offices and city halls are usually intended to be beautiful or at least impressive. This is not generally the case with industrial buildings and premises because, consciously or unconsciously, less consideration was being given to the aesthetics of the buildings erected for industrial purposes. It is hardly surprising that this in turn influences the way the worker sees himself, his workplace, and the interaction between the two.

The same applies to the more immediate environment of the individual worker. The physical design of the workplace can obstruct communication between fellow workers (distance, walls). This may decrease group cohesion and support, while safety requirements are easily threatened. Many jobs are carried out by single workers, isolated from the rest of the community. This easily results in social deprivation. An important element in this is that the worker loses the opportunity to demonstrate to other people his existence and achievements and the quality of his performance. All this can lead to alienation, apathy and mental stress.

The opposite extreme may be equally stressful, namely when the situation is characterised by a total lack of privacy. Here, the worker may be forced to interact with a superabundance of people, without any opportunity to withdraw from communication or conflict even for a short period.

In summary, industrial buildings and premises can have a powerful influence on those working in them, for good and bad. As Sir Winston Churchill put it, "we shape our buildings; thereafter they shape us".

Odours, illumination, climatic factors

Workers frequently attach great importance to _odours_. Although their significance as warning signs of technical incidents must not be overlooked, there is not always a relation between the smell given off by a substance and its possible toxicity (Levi, 1981 b).

Another focus of common complaints concerns insufficient or too strong and, in particular, glaring illumination which may lead not only to fatigue but also to headache, dizziness and an increased accident risk.

A third area of complaint concerns exposure to temperature extremes. The human organism tries to maintain a temperature balance

which heat, radiation, convection and conduction often disturb.
Thus the temperature balance may be disturbed by standing on a cold
concrete floor, sitting on a cold metal chair or handling cold tools.
To some extent, the organism usually adapts to a hot climate, as a
rule, within a couple of weeks.   Adaptation to cold may also occur,
but usually in local tissues only, e.g. by increasing the blood flow
to cold-exposed hands.

Air moisture is of great importance for the experience of
temperature.   Deviations from optimal levels (40 to 60 per cent)
occur in many work environments.   Another important factor concerns
air velocity, which is usually recommended to be 0.2 m/s unless the
temperature is high and greater velocities are preferred.

Whether or not climatic conditions are stress and distress-
producing depends further on the interaction between the heaviness
of the work to be performed, the physical and mental state of the
worker, and existing temperature, humidity and velocity of the
air.

Combined environmental stressors;
reciprocal impact of occupational
and other influences

So far, every type of exposure and its possible effects has
been considered separately.   However, as already indicated,
real-life conditions usually lead to a combination of many
exposures.   These might become superimposed on each other in an
additive way or synergistically.   In this way, the "last straw"
may be a very trivial environmental factor which, however, is
added to the very considerable existing environmental load.

Social structures outside work can influence health and well-
being in the work setting as well as outside it.   For example,
although inadequate housing is in no way the only factor making it
difficult for a shiftworker to sleep during the day, attention to
housing factors may facilitate his going to sleep and staying asleep.
The following are other examples of structural factors outside work,
the effects of which need to be studied and their modification
evaluated (Levi, Frankenhaeuser and Gardell, 1982).

Long distances between workplace and home, as well as inadequate
public transport, force the worker to spend much time in commuting,
often under crowded or otherwise unpleasant conditions that are

difficult to control. Exposure to such conditions has been demonstrated to result in increased adrenaline excretion (Lundberg, 1976; Singer, Lundberg and Frankenhaeuser, 1978).

Insufficient or inadequate day care for pre-school children may add very considerably to the stress experienced by working parents and their children. But the availability of day care is just part of the problem. Its quality is also important, as was shown in one of our studies, in which an increase in the number of nurses per child group was introduced into the psychosocial environment of 100 3-year-old children in ten day-care nurseries. A longitudinal and interdisciplinary evaluation of the effects (Kagan et al., 1978) demonstrated a decrease in child stress in terms of adrenaline excretion and behavioural deviations, as well as in nurse stress, in terms of a sharp decline in absenteeism, with possible secondary beneficial effects on the situation and health of the children's parents.

The design of industrial and office buildings can make it difficult or impossible for handicapped workers to fulfil their duties.

Immigrant workers may experience a cultural shock as well as the usual occupational stressors (ILO, 1974a, b). Ability to cope may be decreased further by insufficient knowledge of the language spoken at work.

Briefly, conditions outside work can influence occupational stress, health and well-being. Similarly, occupational stress can result in a spill-over into the workers' existence outside work. Studies have shown that narrow and socially isolated jobs create passivity or social helplessness. Workers who never participate in planning or decision-making, who rarely co-operate with or talk to other people during the workday, who are doing the same old routine day in and day out, probably learn to act in basically the same way in situations outside work as well. One set of studies shows that when the exercise of discretion in work is curtailed by spatial, temporal or technical restrictions built into the work process, the individual's ability to develop active relations during his spare time will diminish. Persons whose jobs entail serious constraints with respect to autonomy and social interaction at work take far less part in those organised and goal-oriented activities outside work that require planning and co-operation with others (Meissner, 1971; Gardell, 1976; Westlander, 1976).

A representative survey of the Swedish male labour force carried out in 1968 showed that workers doing psychologically unrewarding work took much less part in various organised leisure activities than persons who did not have such jobs.   This finding was especially true for cultural, political and trade union activities of a kind which require active participation and communication with others.   The leisure activities of the workers examined centred on the nuclear family, sports and outdoor life, and the television set (Karasek, 1981).   This study was repeated six years later, in 1974. It was found that those whose jobs had changed during the period to give them a richer job content and a greater say on the job showed increased participation outside the job in voluntary associations, study work and trade union and political activities.   In contrast, those whose jobs during the period had become more narrow and confined owing to the introduction of computers or other forms of rationalisation participated less in such outside activities in 1974 than in 1968 (Karasek, 1981).

THOSE WHO ARE VULNERABLE

3

"One man's meat is another man's poison."   This empirical fact obviously reflects differences in man's psychobiological "programming" resulting from genetic factors and earlier environmental influences.   The latter include both physical and psychosocial stimuli.   The complex pattern of "programming" factors makes every individual unique and determines his propensity to react in one way or another, e.g. in response to various components of the work environment (Levi, 1981b).

Some of the determinants of individual susceptibility are age, sex and present illness or state of chronic disability.   Similarly, group susceptibility may vary, depending upon group cohesion and group support.   In the present context we feel unable to divide humanity into a large number of subgroups, from which predictions could be made in relation to general or specific vulnerability to potentially noxious influences in the industrial setting.   Only five broad categories will be mentioned in more detail, namely very young workers, older workers, migrant workers, handicapped workers, and pregnant women workers.

Coping strategies

Before discussing these categories, however, we should mention that potentially pathogenic reactions, particularly to psychosocial stimuli, are heavily influenced by the individual's ability to cope (Lazarus, 1966, 1976).   Facing a threatening situation (e.g. exposure to an occupational health risk or the risk of unemployment) some people resort to denial.   They "refuse" to perceive a threat considered by others to be quite obvious.   If this psychological defence mehanism is effective, peace of body and mind may be preserved

temporarily even in the face of what objectively would be considered
as dramatic calamities.   On the other hand, in the long run, the
effects of such an ostrich-like policy may become disastrous.

Another example of coping mechanisms is intellectualisation.
Here, the individual or group is trying to calculate the risk in
almost statistical terms ("Why should this happen to me?").   Others
resort to magical or dogmatic thinking, whereas others again make use
of "displacement", focusing on rather trivial risks and stressors,
thereby decreasing their awareness of much more serious threats.

An additional coping strategy consists in actively trying to
find out as much as possible about the threatening situation and
attempting to gain control over it.   In other cases, coping means
accepting and trying to tolerate the inevitable.   "What cannot be
cured must be endured."

Young workers

The term "young worker" refers to youth of both sexes who are
admitted to employment but are covered by special provisions of
labour legislation.   Depending on the laws and regulations in force,
the age group is 15-20 years (in some cases 14-18, in others 15-21,
as in the ILO's Model code of safety regulations for industrial
establishments;   see also ILO, 1977b).

As pointed out by Forssman and Coppée (1975), approximately
10 per cent of the world's population consists of young people
between 15 and 20 years old.   A much greater proportion of the
world's population is under 15 years of age.   In developing
countries, this age group accounts for an estimated 42 per cent and
in developed countries for 27 per cent of the population.   Because
of present sharp decreases in infant and child mortality, this will
have a dramatic secondary influence on the age distribution of
tomorrow when these children reach reproductive age.   Already today,
a number of countries are unable to provide adequate vocational training for many young persons or for that matter any useful employment
for many of those who are old enough to work.   This situation is
one of the most serious problems confronting these countries and the
international community at large.   The situation is further complicated by the fact that many young persons leave the countryside to
seek their fortunes in the cities and towns even if the prospects
there are too minimal.   In the urban context, they frequently

experience the greatest difficulties in finding work, are likely to
be exploited, and are constantly threatened by poverty and disease
(see also Mendelievich, 1979; Rodgers and Standing, 1981).

But there are additional problems. Forssman and Coppée draw
attention to the fact that millions of children who should be at
school or at play are at work, sometimes even before their seventh
or eighth birthday. In several countries, children account for up
to 10 per cent of the working population. All this has its roots
in poverty and the lack of schools.

All this leads to much human suffering. Needless to say, all
these problems cannot easily be solved. Our point, however, is
that unless many approaches to the solution of these problems are
combined, traditional approaches to the occupational problems of
young workers will be like chipping away at the rust as the boat
goes down.

Older workers

Life expectancy has increased progressively. In the developed
countries, the average life expectancy at birth is now 72 years.
In the developing world, the figures are lower, being somewhat over
60 years in Latin America, around 49-75 years in Asia and 44-58
years in Africa. The overall trend has meant that the proportion
of the entire population approaching or reaching what is generally
considered to be retirement age has increased and is now considerable
(Levi, 1981b).

As in the case of infants and children, workers belonging to
this age group are at risk for two reasons which often concur.
First, higher age usually enhances general vulnerability and may be
accompanied by an increased incidence of disability in the form of
blindness, hearing impairments, paralysis, impairment or loss of
extremities, etc. Second, many older workers simply have to work
if they are to survive at all, particularly in urban slums where the
risk of exploitation is great, where exposure to noxious stimuli is
high and where protection is low or absent.

Here too the problems must be approached by a combination of
strategies and on several levels. Unless the macro level (provision
of suitable work) receives adequate attention, the micro level
(ergonomic adaptation of work tasks and work endurance) will be of
little importance for the final outcome in terms of health and

physical, mental and social well-being.   Obviously, both levels
deserve attention.

If adjustments are made for regional differences, it can be
generally assumed (Bolinder, 1974) that middle-aged and older workers
should be protected from heavy physical workloads, since as people
get older there is a decline in their capacity for perceiving and
evaluating a pattern of simultaneous and complex signals and for
rapid decision-making based on such evaluations.   On the other hand,
these negative factors are more or less balanced by their higher
degree of knowledge and experience (which, however, may have become
obsolete) and by their greater loyalty and feelings of responsibility.
Unfortunately, the general trend in industrial development is for a
decrease in the number of occupational tasks where such benefits can
be utilised and the drawbacks of the older worker play only a minor
role.

Migrant workers

According to Zwingmann and Pfister-Ammende (1973), "more than
100 million people of the northern hemisphere left their homeland or
were forcefully separated from it" during the first half of the
twentieth century.   They migrated, they were displaced or deported,
they fled from persecution.   The authors summarise the classifica-
tion of the motivations for the move as follows:

(a) physical: e.g. war or natural calamities, such as earthquakes,
     drought, famine, floods, climate, etc.;

(b) economic: e.g. underemployment, low material living standards,
     absence of social security, move ordered by government (flooding
     areas related to dam construction) - industrialisation and
     urbanisation, advanced social security benefits, etc.;

(c) social: family trouble, housing and occupational difficulties -
     future of children, attraction by relatives or friends already
     moved;

(d) psychological: personal conflict, escapism, restlessness,
     difficulties of adjustment to existing society, fear of
     persecution or war - transcultural interest, sense of adventure;

(e) religious: religious intolerance - religious freedom;

(f) political: discrimination, persecution - political ambition;

(g) professional: e.g. inadequate pay, inadequate research
     facilities, etc.

In many instances, the migrant worker has to adapt to a wide variety of new conditions, including differences in climate, eating habits, social customs, cost of living, housing facilities, and type and rhythm of work. He may be handicapped in dealing with these changes by his inexperience of urban life and by his inadequate knowledge of the language of the country. His cultural background, customs and traditions often create a barrier to his integration in the host country. Such factors have an important influence on the migrant worker's behaviour and can predispose him to ill health. The prevalence of psychiatric disorders seems to be two to three times as high among recent migrants as among the local population. Psychosocial stresses may manifest themselves in various physical disorders, particularly of the digestive system. Acute psychotic states or paranoid reactions may appear during the first years of residence in the host countries.

In studies in the host countries, it was found that the accident rate is 2.5 times as high in migrant workers as in nationals. The occupational accident rate was found to be 92 per 1,000 foreign workers, compared with 32 per 1,000 native workers. The annual incidence of industrial accidents was 15.8 per cent among migrant workers as against 10.5 per cent for nationals (WHO, 1976).

In summary, then, there is abundant evidence that migrant workers are a high-risk group deserving special attention which, again, should include ergonomic elements as important components in a comprehensive holistic and ecological programme of prevention of their mental stress in industry (ILO, 1979a, b).

Handicapped workers

A fourth group at risk is much more complex and difficult to define. This is due to the fact that a handicap should always be considered in relation to the work in which the individual is expected to function. As the environmental setting varies enormously not only from community to community but also from one industry to another, the importance of any single handicap or pattern of handicaps will differ according to the environmental opportunities and demands and compensatory potentials in the individual (Levi, 1970, 1981b). Suffice it to say that hundreds of millions of people are severely physically, mentally or socially handicapped. Examples of such groups are the blind, the deaf, the disabled, the mentally retarded or ill, the drug addicts and alcoholics and the refugees. In highly developed countries one may also focus on other "lesser" social handicaps. In many developing countries this is next to impossible in view of the enormous poverty, the apathy (imposed or otherwise) of many of the underprivileged and the lack of social and medical services.

It follows that the handicapped constitute a high-risk group even in highly developed countries. More often than not, they remain unemployed (although many get sheltered employment). In developing countries this is so to an even higher degree, and their fate depends almost entirely on group cohesion and family support. When such means of support tend to fail, e.g. because of extreme poverty, social disorganisation and the dissolution of families by urbanisation and migration, the quality of life of the handicapped will necessarily be close to nil.

Again, the increased vulnerability often coincides with an increased exposure to the most vicious environments. Noise, pollution, overcrowding, nutritional deficiencies and low hygienic standards characterise some huge industrial as well as settlement areas not only in the developing countries but also in the slums of many developed countries. To these very areas, various segregational forces "sort out" exactly those individuals who are most in need of a more favourable environment. In this way, maximal vulnerability is combined with maximal exposure to environmental stressors, increasing the risk of a subsequent decline in health and well-being below the subsistence level.

Women workers

As pointed out by Shalit (1977), most countries have had and many still have labour regulations which forbid the employment of women in certain jobs. This seems to be caused by three factors: the lower physical strength of women; the desire by women or men to protect home and family life; and the desire to protect pregnant women, particularly during the early stages of pregnancy (Hunt, 1975). The second of these factors is conditioned by social norms and reflects society's concept of "what is right for a woman to do". The other two, however, are based on physiological evidence.

One additional obstacle that easily creates mental stress in women is the fact that many women, in addition to working full time, also have to carry the burden of the full responsibility for housework and/or rearing of the children. In extreme cases this means that women may have to work more or less without interruption for, say, 16 hours a day, seven days a week.

The only obvious factor that undoubtedly leads to increased vulnerability in the female relates to pregnancy. Pregnant women, or rather their foetuses, run special risks when they are exposed to, for instance, ionising radiations, toxic chemicals, vibrations and arduous physical effort. Apart from these cases, however, there is nothing to prove that women are more sensitive than men to harmful substances and the onslaughts of the environment (ILO, 1976a, b; Hunt, 1975).

HOW TO PREVENT AND TO TREAT

4

"An ounce of prevention

        ... is worth a pound of cure." Unfortunately, however, occu-
pational health services today are mainly concerned with interventions
against precursors of disease or against disease itself, i.e. usually
at a stage where functional disturbances or structural injuries have
already occurred. If, for example, a very monotonous but attention-
demanding work situation has provoked a gastritis or a peptic ulcer,
occupational health officers intervene with hydrochloric acid
neutralisers and with drugs that inhibit the increased flow of
impulses from the brain to the stomach and the duodenum. If fear
of becoming redundant and sacked provokes palpitations of the heart,
we block the flow of impulses from the brain to the heart by means
of adrenergic beta receptor blockers, or else we intervene in the
cerebral processes by administering tranquillisers to counteract
anxiety. These methods are not readily dispensed with and should
definitely not be underrated, especially when a disease or disability
has already developed. It is important, however, to apply measures
of prevention as well as of therapy, not only at the mechanism level
but also with regard to possible causes in the work situation
(Levi, 1981b).

        Is it possible, for instance, to change (i.e. improve) our
working environment? Is it possible to alter our experience and
appreciation of that environment, for instance by instilling us with
realistic expectations? Can the "psychobiological programming" be
influenced in a favourable direction so that the propensity for
pathogenic reactions declines - for instance by means of physical
exercise, various relaxation techniques, healthy dietary and sleeping habits, etc.? Intervention at the mechanism level using drugs

has already been mentioned. Perhaps, intervention of this kind
could be supplemented by psychotherapy? By counselling? By help-
ing people to change their own working conditions, resolve their own
conflicts and cope with their own problems? By giving them a chance
to talk things over with somebody who has time to listen?

Would it not be worth while to try to nip various diseases in
the bud by identifying and promptly treating their precursors or
early stages? Can improvements to the environment <u>outside</u> working
life serve to strengthen resistance to or provide compensation for
those strains of the working environment which simply cannot be
avoided? Is it possible to protect the vulnerable by endeavouring
to put "the right man in the right place"?

Strategies for change in the working environment

As to the mechanisms by which changes in environmental conditions
should be brought about, at work and elsewhere, a main issue is how
to increase, organise and vitalise the workers' (and citizens') own
resources. The workers themselves constitute a key resource in
identifying hazards at the workplace, on their own or with the aid
of scientifically trained consultants working on their behalf. To
facilitate this, and to ensure that action can be taken, there is a
need for instruments such as <u>legislation</u> based on and combined with
research (Levi, Frankenhaeuser and Gardell, 1982). Empirical data
show that work stress may cause problems in two different ways:
first, since there may be a direct relation between certain objective
conditions at work, on the one hand, and physiological and psychological stress and ill health, on the other; second, since certain
work conditions may create fatigue and/or passivity in the individual
and thus make him less prone to involve himself actively in attempts
to change working conditions and behaviour that may be detrimental
to his health.

It follows that action is needed at the individual level as well
as at systems level, such as organisational and technological design
(Gardell, 1980; Levi, 1981b). Work at the <u>individual</u> level
ties easily into traditional medical thinking such as promoting
sensible health behaviour, such as non-smoking, non-drinking, diet,
physical exercise, pace slowdown, etc. Also, at this level, one
finds remedies, such as retraining, replacement into other types of
job, etc. Prevention at the <u>systems</u> level is much more difficult

and controversial, and there are no generally accepted ways of dealing with the problems. Available experience indicates a need for public intervention, the creation of public resources, and the development of strategies at the enterprise level.

The effectiveness of government intervention depends, in part, on national institutional traditions. Legislation is a means of providing statutory authority to employers and workers to act in certain areas and in certain directions. Rules and regulations related to the work environment may be designed to facilitate identification of certain types of problems and certain types of remedies to be applied. This is evident, for instance, in the Swedish and the Norwegian Working Environment Acts, most clearly though in the Norwegian Act. Government intervention may also mean that money and knowledge are made available to the companies for environmental changes, for research purposes and for information and training activities.

At the enterprise level, the main issue seems to be how to increase and organise worker protection. Here, most countries seem to rely upon trade unions and the development of negotiating machinery to deal with health hazards in the workplace. In this way, worker representatives can be given certain rights and means, regulated by laws, in order to act effectively on behalf of their colleagues. They may, for instance, be given the right to have a say in organisational and technological design, in decisions on equipment, on work methods, on the use of certain types of materials and products, on personnel policies and so on. They may further be given the right to stop dangerous work, to call in experts to help to make assessments or to conduct research on their behalf, at costs paid by production or by government funds created for such purposes. There is a variety of organisational solutions to these problems in the various European countries with widely differing levels of ambition.

To organise worker protection in this way is important and necessary but not enough. It is also very important, though perhaps more difficult, to try to find means to stimulate workers in general, i.e. the "grass-roots" themselves, to take care of their own problems. As indicated earlier, narrow and system-paced jobs for workers who have little say in management decisions may eventually create worker attitudes that are passive and alienated even to exposure to serious occupational health hazards. Therefore, awareness must be increased among them and competence and power extended

to <u>the workers themselves</u> to help them to identify and change un-
healthy working conditions.   This has been the goal of recent
Scandinavian legislation.

In Sweden the Working Environment Act, 1977 (see below),
stresses the importance of <u>personal</u> control over the work situation,
whereas the Act respecting Co-determination at Work (1976) stresses
the influence of workers <u>as a group</u>.   On the basis of these two
Acts, fundamental changes in working life might be accomplished.

These aims are shared by the <u>Norwegian Working Environment Act</u>,
which expresses the following provisions:

    (1) <u>General requirements</u>.   Technology, work organisation, work
time (e.g. shift plans) and payment systems are to be
designed so that negative physiological or psychological
effects for employees are avoided as well as negative
influences on the alertness necessary to the observance of
safety considerations.   Employees are to be given possibilities for personal development and for the maintenance
and development of skills.

    (2) <u>Design of jobs</u>.   In the planning of work and design of
jobs, possibilities for employee self-determination and
maintenance of skills are to be considered.   Monotonous
repetitive work and work that is bound by machine or
assembly line, in such a way that no room is left for
variation in work rhythm, should be avoided.   Jobs should
be designed so as to give possibilities for variation, for
contact with others, for understanding of the inter-
dependence between elements that constitute a job, and
for information and feedback to employees concerning
production requirements and results.

    (3) <u>Systems for planning and control (e.g. automatic data
processing systems)</u>.   Workers or their elected representatives are to be kept informed about systems used for
planning and control and any changes in such systems.
They are to be given the training necessary to understand
the systems and to influence their design.

    (4) <u>Mode of remuneration and risk to safety</u>.   Piece-rate
payment and related forms of payment are not to be used if
salaried systems can increase the safety level.

As mentioned above, the <u>Swedish</u> legislative approach is twofold.
The Working Environment Act, 1977, which came into force on 1 July
1978 is an open-frame law with general statements, such as "working
conditions shall be adapted to human physical and mental aptitudes"
and "an effort shall be made to arrange the work in such a way that
an employee can himself influence his work situation".   This frame-
work is complemented by specifications from two sources: the National
Board of Occupational Safety and Health (1980), and (perhaps even
more important for mental health purposes) the Act respecting

Co-determination at Work, dated 10 June 1976. The latter Act requires that information be given to workers' organisations on all matters and at all levels about working conditions. It entitles local unions to negotiate on any matter that may influence their job situation. The parties themselves - the employers and workers at the local plants - shall agree on the job specifications they consider suitable. In order to guide local action, the Swedish Trade Union Confederation has endorsed a special action programme on psychosocial aspects of the working environment (LO, 1980).

Whether these laws and related recommendations will be success-ful remains to be seen. There is no doubt that they are far-sighted but they are also not very specific. The general intent of the law is given but offences are not specified. Much will depend on how they are used and what costs are attached to effective remedies.

How can harmful stress be cured?

There are three basic paths to follow in treating stress symptoms. Where possible, we should eliminate the stress-producing situation or remove the individual from it, i.e. either clean up the working environment, offer the individual special protection, or endeavour to find him another job. When this cannot be done, one can seek to influence the psychological processes and related physical symptoms by means of drugs (pharmacotherapy) or psycho-therapy. Another possibility is to improve resistance through exercise, physical training and relaxation, meditation, etc. Of course, none of these possibilities rules out the others.

Pharmacotherapy employs drugs which act on the cerebral sites of mental functions, thereby indirectly affecting the organ symptoms that accompany these functions; other drugs affect the stream of impulses in the sympathetic and parasympathetic nervous systems to the various organs. These drugs often help considerably. But while they can modify a person's reactions to various stressors, they can never resolve deeper psychological conflicts.

In psychotherapy the doctor employs conversations and other forms of mental influence in an attempt to change those injurious habits of mind and ways of responding which predispose a person to experience stress in various situations later in life. The most developed form of psychotherapy is psychoanalysis, which is time-consuming and expensive. It is necessary in only a relatively limited number of cases.

Exercise and physical training are probably of use because they
help to expend the pent-up energy produced by stress.   Instead of
striking your boss or running away from your wife, you kick a foot-
ball or go for a run.   The pent-up tension leaks away.   The increased heart work and higher blood lipid content are put to good use.

There are further several relaxation methods, autogenic training,
etc., that can be used to reduce the body's propensity to react with
stress and, indeed, to mitigate stress reactions themselves.

Psychological first aid

Most of us are able to treat a surface graze or scratch.
Similarly, everyone can and should be able to administer the simplest
form of mental assistance for which the industrial psychiatrist
Erland Mindus has coined the term "psychological first-aid poultice".

Such a poultice is easy to apply.   The basic point is to give
the person who needs help a chance to speak his mind;   just being
able to do this is a great relief for most people.   Once they have
been put into words, problems gain structure and become less vague
and terrifying.   On the other hand, one should be very sparing with
"good advice" for this calls for a much more thorough knowledge of
the patient's situation than laymen in general possess.   The best
help one can offer is, quite simply, to listen and, when applicable,
to offer social and practical support.

For the friend or relative of a stressed person, for his super-
visor and mates on the job, it will, in addition, be useful to keep
the following in mind:

(a)   Remember that a person with psychosomatic or psychiatric symptoms
       is not imagining them.   He may suffer and be just as incapaci-
       tated as other persons who are ailing.   Show understanding.

(b)   Don't tell a person that he should "take hold of himself",
       "shape up", etc.   Try to help him to help himself.

(c)   Show consideration and do not be too hard on those who are
       especially prone to depression, fatigue and anxiety.   Very
       often, a change of scenery within the firm can spare the
       sufferer unnecessary strain and friction.

(d)   Show an interest in problems of those under you or of your
       colleagues.   Let them speak their minds if they wish, but do
       not begin to diagnose and hand out treatment yourself.   Damage
       is easily done.

The practical advice that one can give to trade unions, occupational safety organisations, labour leaders and management is that they treat seriously all reports of subjective stress reactions and ill health as described above.   If complaints of and/or absenteeism for psychological and psychosomatic ailments are considerable, personnel turnover high and job satisfaction inadequate, the next step is to determine (by means of interviews and questionnaires) in what job environments these things occur.   A third step would be to discuss the findings of environmental and health problems, and their inter-relations, with the workers concerned, propose environmental improvements at work jointly with them and with management, and make trial alterations to these environmental factors in what may reasonably be assumed to be a positive direction.   A fourth step would be to determine whether this, indeed, improves health, job satisfaction, etc.   Later on, the new knowledge may be applied on a broader scale and the application evaluated.   This way of monitoring and improving psychosocial work environment and workers' health is already being applied in e.g. the Volvo Automobile Company, the Swedish construction industry, and in some Swedish governmental agencies.

PRINCIPLES OF PREVENTION OF STRESS-RELATED DISEASES

5

According to the Swedish Secretariat for Futurological Studies (1978), social expenditures in Sweden quadrupled in constant prices from 1930 to 1945 and rose more than sixfold from 1950 to 1975. Despite this expansion of costs and resources, the general health of the population did not improve. Here as elsewhere, what is lacking is a comprehensive plan for the design and provision of social and health care - including occupational health care - in the light of human needs. In plain terms, social and health care - generally and with regard to the work setting - must be adapted to the consumer, in our case to the worker (Levi, 1981c).

The task is made more difficult by the fact that occupational health problems are almost never simple. Each problem has many causes and ties in with many other problems. It is clear, for instance, that occupational health problems, financial problems, child care problems, environmental problems, housing problems, problems of law and order, communications problems, and so on, are all intertwined. An effective solution must tackle the entire set of problems as an inter-related whole, requiring a co-ordinated set of measures. One and the same ailing older worker is seen as a problem of medication by a heart specialist, a problem of work environment planning by an ergonomist, an economic problem by management and by a social worker, and a problem of attitudes and group dynamics by a psychologist. All are right, but none is entirely right. The problem can be solved effectively only if its various interpretations and remedies are co-ordinated. Such solutions are difficult to implement. Every specialisation, every group of experts and every administrative body protects its own field and tends to disregard others. Politicians, too, set to work more as specialists than as co-ordinators and "general practitioners".

Occupational health and well-being depend on isolated, individual, easily delimitable causal factors just as little as do work-related illness and suffering. Rather, they depend on a complicated interplay between man and his environment, at work and outside it. Some factors in this interplay are essential conditions for health (or ill health). Others may be contributory but not essential or sufficient. Health care and environmental protection, in the occupational setting and in general, must therefore be focused on a multiplicity of interacting factors and events to achieve the fullest preventive and therapeutic effect and avoid the creation of new problems.

For the planning for better occupational health and well-being to be effective, there are five principles to observe:

(1) Planning must take place in collaboration with those immediately affected, that is, it must be participatory. The workers for whom it is meant must be given the necessary opportunity and competence and be encouraged to take part themselves, both in making and in implementing decisions to improve work environment and occupational health and well-being.

(2) The measures must cover all the relevant aspects and be well co-ordinated. For example, planning for workers' health, well-being, personal development and self-realisation is a task not just for occupational health authorities and a few psycho-social experts but also for the authorities responsible for planning industrial buildings and premises, planning national economy and investments, educational planning, city planning, public health planning, etc., and all these activities must be co-ordinated.

(3) Integrated planning is necessary throughout: planning must be co-ordinated at the international, national and local levels, and between these levels.

(4) Planning must be continuous, that is, plans must be constantly improved and adapted in accordance with any new knowledge that experience may bring or with what technological and societal development make necessary. Planning must give consideration to both short and long-term goals, as well as means and resources.

(5) The planning process must include feedback with continuous assessment, not only in economic terms but also in terms of health and well-being. Problems are constantly changing. A problem may be solved but this does not mean that it will stay solved.

Thus, the key words are: co-operation, co-ordination, integration, continuity, evaluation (cf. Ackoff, 1974, 1976).

Proposed guide-lines for long-term
planning of working environment,
health and health care

In the light of what has been said, the following guide-lines
should be considered in the prevention of stress-related illness in
industry and the promotion of occupational health and well-being
(Levi, 1981b, c).

1.   Clearly specified objectives

One fundamental question concerns the critically important but
commonly neglected problem of what we want with our society and our
industrial, environmental, social and health policies.   There has
long been an inclination to stress quantity at the expense of quality,
the technical and the economic at the cost of the human.   However,
more and more people have come to realise that objectives must first
and foremost be formulated in human terms, i.e. in terms to do with the
quality of life.   Some of the key ingredients of this concept are
human health and well-being, personal development and self-
realisation.   It should be the overriding goal, openly stated, of
every country's and every community's occupational, social and
environmental policy.   To achieve this, working life, comprising
production of goods and services and creation of wealth, is an
important tool.

Thus, having decided what kind of life and society we actually
want (and do not want), we find it easier to strive actively to
achieve this in the most effective way.   This implies that occupational, environmental, economic, social and health policy must not
be satisfied merely with increasing wealth and endeavouring to
mitigate injurious effects but should also attempt to get at the
causes of such effects and promote the quality of working life.

2.   The holistic, ecological and
systems approach

The problems with regard to the work environment, content and
organisation of work and to work-related ill health have a multiplicity of causes which themselves interact.   No analysis of such
problems can be effective without a holistic (comprehensive) approach.
Further, no attempt to solve these problems can hope to have the

intended effect without a holistic approach in outlining pertinent measures and evaluating their outcome.

The structures of working life and other social systems are divisible but their functions are not. Unless the various functions are well co-ordinated - and they are not today - the result is a number of isolated activities - e.g. aiming at promoting productivity, wealth, health, etc. - each well planned in itself, which fail to yield what the planners and executors expect and the working population has a right to demand.

In addition, one and the same phenomenon, or one and the same result of the measures undertaken, may be both beneficial and deleterious, namely for different groups and/or in different respects. What is beneficial for young, healthy and well-off workers is not necessarily so for those who are in various respects underprivileged. What is advantageous from a strictly economic point of view may be costly in other terms, for example with regard to health and well-being and vice versa.

Consider the following goals: jobs should be sufficient in number and diversity; wages should be high, fair and rapidly increasing in real terms; workers should be protected against pollution and accidents; goods and services should be of high quality and reasonably priced; there must be a sufficient number of nurseries, schools, health centres, care centres for the aged, cultural institutions, etc., and moreover they must be easily accessible. All well and good: but no measure should be planned independently. Each must be weighed against and co-ordinated with all the others. Economy, housing, work, travel, education, cultural facilities, law enforcement and other social functions cannot be planned separately. They must be planned as part of an integrated whole (Levi, 1981b, c).

Our society has moved towards increasingly extreme sectorisation. This is true of both occupational and social planning and individual care. Occupational environmental questions fall under the jurisdiction of one authority, while another handles the consequences of such influences on health. It would be more efficient to regard the individual, the group and the environment as components in a system in which each is affected by the others in many ways. Although rather self-evident, this "systems" approach is not practised today. It requires a new way of thinking in industrial and social planning, environmental conservation and individual care.

Thus the administration of occupational health care may involve
ensuring that the work environment is free of noxious substances,
counteracting destructive life-styles, teaching the employees good
eating habits, making sure that the workplace environment and the
content and organisation of work promote health and well-being
instead of impairing them, and that housing and leisure time are
enriching and favour good health.   It follows from this that occupational health care is a matter of concern for many occupational
groups beyond the strictly medical occupations and eventually for
the individuals themselves.

3.   Feedback and assessment:
     Learning from experience

Occupational environmental and health policy decisions, if well
planned, will be based on available information and, in addition, on
a notion of how society, working life and life in general should be
shaped.   However, even well-intentioned and apparently well-founded
decisions can prove to have negative side-effects which are difficult
to foresee.   The safeguard against seriously wrong decisions lies
in a continuous and comprehensive appraisal of decisions once taken
and of other social developments.   This can be made possible, for
example, by a general rule that 1 to 2 per cent of the costs for
introducing changes in the work environment or in the content and
organisation of work must be earmarked for interdisciplinary, long-
term evaluation of their effects.

4.   Democratisation and activation

Political systems vary considerably in their trust in the
individual worker, his judgement and his sagacity.   In many
countries this trust is considerable.   At the same time it is
obvious that many industries are becoming increasingly complex.
Specialists have developed in practically every service area, every
aspect of life, and for every bodily function.   Many people have
come to believe that they have neither sufficient understanding nor
the capacity and opportunity to take care of themselves and each
other, even when they do in fact possess the necessary qualifications,
or can acquire them relatively easily.

In many areas, specialists have successively assumed many of
the functions which formerly people fulfilled independently within
the workplace, extended family or neighbourhood.   Some of the
support, encouragement and feelings of "belonging" which workers

and supervisors could and should give their fellow workers is now
increasingly in the hands of professionally trained personnel.
Minor physical and mental problems and ailments - one's own and
others - which people used to treat themselves on the basis of
experience, are now in the hands of a complicated and increasingly
more expensive and more impersonal medical care system.   Solidarity
with other human beings has definitely increased in some countries,
but only in terms of fiscal policy.   At the personal level it has,
if anything, diminished.   The extended hand to a fellow worker,
a fellow human being in need of help, has been replaced by a larger
contribution to local or national taxes.   Instead of devoting time
and sympathy to a person who needs someone to speak to, we provide
tax revenue to pay for social workers and psychiatrists.   These
services are necessary but they do not replace personal attention.
Obviously, both kinds of solidarity and concern are required.   But
the way things are going, human sympathy is becoming increasingly a
function of persons who are hired and trained for the task for which
they receive contractual salaries.

This does not mean, of course, that specialists are becoming
superfluous or that representative democracy has had its day.   But
it does mean that individuals should not be divorced from responsibility for, and having a direct influence on, a number of important
aspects of life, such as working life and occupational health;   on the
contrary, employees should have their own competence increasingly
expanded through education and information, and their self-confidence
and initiative should be restored by broadening their awareness and
giving them incentives and power.   Human sympathy and decision-
making have become much too institutionalised, centralised and
tagged with professional labels.   This is no way for a vital
democracy to function.   It requires the engagement of all, in
personal matters as well as in matters of public concern (Levi,
1981c).

5.   Individualisation

In a highly centralised society it is tempting to assume that
all workers have approximately the same abilities and needs, since
this makes the central planning of occupational health care, of the
occupational environment and of service facilities so much easier.
In a more decentralised and smaller-scale society, there is the same
respect for the equal worth of all individuals, but greater flexi-
bility in planning, with allowance made for the differing abilities
and needs of all.   Both preventive and therapeutic efforts can in

this way be provided for those who need them most.   In this way, the limited network of occupational safety and health services becomes dense, where the needs are greatest and where it confers maximum benefit.

6.   Preventing harm and promoting
      health and well-being

Prevention is better than cure, but if a cure is required, it is better done on dry land than in midstream.   However, for damage that exists, society invests considerable resources and increases them from year to year.   As mentioned above, the Swedish Secretariat for Futurological Studies quite correctly points out that these enormous investments have by no means led to improved mental and physical health in the past decade as reflected in a decreased utilisation of health care services.   Part of the reason for this may be that groups of individuals who formerly needed but had no access to various forms of social services now have that access. Even so, the time has clearly come to rethink and restructure priorities in favour of disease prevention and health promotion as important complements to relief and cure.

The final report of the National Swedish Health Social Welfare Board's Work Group for Mental Health Protection and Promotion (1978) outlined different levels on which such preventive measures should take place:

(a)   on structural macro level (for example improved content and
       organisation of work in the entire nation, improved forms of
       collaboration and employee co-determination) usually through
       legislation or collective bargaining;

(b)   on the structural micro level (for example by improving work
       environment in a certain specific factory, office or enterprise);

(c)   on the level of increasing resistance to illness in individual
       workers (increasing social competence, health promotion,
       training in coping and conflict resolution, etc.);

(d)   on the level of adaptation to reality (realistic expectations
       as to supervisor, fellow workers, work content, salary, etc.);

(e)   on the level of getting "the right job for the right person" in
       a pluralistic society (e.g. vocational guidance);

(f)   on the level of crisis intervention and "buffering" social
       support during critical periods, especially for high-risk
       groups;

(g) on the level of increasing power and competence to individual
workers to cope with their own and each other's problems.

Most important is to integrate the planning and execution of
measures for promoting occupational health and preventing work-
related and other diseases (and hence improving the quality of life)
on all these levels.   To decide on such measures on structural
levels is a task for politicians, management and labour unions.
However, individual workers and groups of employees can and should,
to varying degrees, also make an important and sometimes decisive
contribution.

7.   Utilisation of existing knowledge

One of the basic weaknesses in today's occupational environmental
and health policy is the insufficient and unsystematic utilisation of
the experience and "know-how" that has already been accumulated
through research and development.   In the area of improving work
environment and organisation and the content of work, in particular,
it often takes a long time for the results of research to be
implemented in practical activity.   There are several reasons for
this.   It is very difficult to obtain an overview of all relevant
knowledge, for one thing because it exists in many languages, in many
branches of science, and in many data bases.   Further, there is a
tendency rather to produce new knowledge than to integrate and
utilise existing material.   Another difficulty is that scientific
language is often incomprehensible to management and unions, and even
to decision-makers of various kinds and to specialists in other
areas.   The investment in creating new knowledge (research) has been
incomparably greater than the investment in processes of integration,
translation and utilisation of existing knowledge, and this has been
detrimental to the practical usefulness of this enormous accumulation
of scientific information.   This is a strong argument for much
closer collaboration between research, on the one hand, and central
and local authorities, management and labour unions and occupational
health workers, on the other.   ILO, WHO, the newly formed Section of
Occupational Psychiatry of the World Psychiatric Association, the
International Commission for Occupational Mental Health, and others,
are all actively promoting such a development.

Researchers should be confronted with the practical problems of
working life and with the priorities of the "consumers".   Politicians, management and labour unions in their turn should be
informed about the possibilities and limitations of research so that
they can ask reasonable questions in problem areas to which they
attach high priority.   It then becomes the task of the researchers,

in collaboration with documentation and information specialists,
and client representatives, to work jointly to compile the knowledge
that exists, create new knowledge and, where possible, to put forward
suggestions for solutions to problems in terms comprehensible to
their "consumers".   These compilations and recommendations would
then function as a basis for making subsequent democratic and
administrative decisions.   An important component in such a process
is the feedback of knowledge to the workers themselves, for example
through the mass media.

8.   Integrated monitoring of
      environment, health and
      well-being

To be able to identify in time the risk factors in the working
environment and their negative health effects, a continuous monitoring is necessary, including integrated occupational environment and
health statistics (WHO, 1973; Kagan and Levi, 1974;)

Many authorities in every country collect statistical information, each for their own purpose.   Much of this activity has
probably become an end in itself, while few attempts are made to
describe events in the occupational environment, in our social life
and in occupational and public health in such a way that disturbing
trends may be discovered and preventive measures or measures to
heighten preparedness are taken;   correlations between different
environmental factors, on the one hand (for example industrial
hazards, working environment, travel times, workplaces, socio-
economic factors) and social and health factors, on the other (for
example various kinds of occupational diseases and work accidents,
general morbidity and mortality) can be recorded;   and the effects
of various occupational environment, social and health measures may
be assessed (for example the efforts of regional policy, population
redistributions, changes with regard to the content and organisation
of work, new approaches to employee co-determination and participation, etc.).   This collection of occupational environment and health
data must take place at group level only and in such a way that the
integrity of the individual is not jeopardised.

Thus what we need is a system for such integrated monitoring.
Let me stress expressly that data must be gathered at group level,
and not at individual level, and that data gathering should be
premised on a holistic view of the employees and their working life
and hence include not only physical and chemical environmental factors

at the workplace and in other environments but also psychosocial and socio-economic factors. Correspondingly, the "effect side of the ledger" should include not only morbidity and mortality of various physical diseases but also various psychological and social phenomena and the components of what is commonly referred to as the "quality of life" (Levi, 1981b).

9. Meeting the need for new
    knowledge

One of the major obstacles to an optimal occupational environment and health policy is the fact that the causal links between occupational environmental factors, on the one hand, and negative social and health phenomena in the workers, on the other, are very incompletely known. Consequently, there is a great need for research efforts, both basic and of a more applied kind. We have already pointed out the importance of conducting research in close contact with the recipients of its benefits. Thus the problem is partly organisational; but it is also, and importantly, a question of resources. It is especially curious that problem areas in occupational health, where problems and countermeasures cost hundreds and thousand hundreds of millions of dollars annually (depending, inter alia, on the size of the country), get only a few millions for research, despite the large and important gaps in our knowledge here. Research can close many of these gaps and thus point the way to better solutions to the problems. It can also help to assess existing preventive and therapeutic measures (Levi, 1979; Kagan and Levi, 1974; Elliott and Eisdorfer, 1982).

Such assessments should include what in Sweden is called social review. Some steps in this direction have already been taken. In our view, such activity should be introduced gradually into all areas of practical, occupational, social, health and environmental policy and especially into all new ones.

Of course, needs will vary from country to country: for such preventive planning - to include the formulation of aims, the practical application of existing "know-how", integrated occupational environment and health monitoring, stimulation to individual initiative, power and competence, evaluation and research - should constitute the foundation for occupational environmental and health policy of the future.

REFERENCES

Abercrombie, M.L.J.   1976.   "Architecture: Psychological aspects",
in Krauss, S. (ed.): Encyclopaedic handbook of medical psychology.
London, Butterworth.

Ackoff, R.L.   1974.   Redesigning the future: A systems approach
to societal problems. New York, Wiley.

---.   1976.   "Does quality of life have to be quantified?", in
Operational Research Quarterly, Vol. 27, No. 2, p. 289.

Ahlbom, A.; Karasek, R.; Theorell, T.   1977.   "Psychosocial
occupational demands and risk for cardio-vascular death", in
Lakartidningen, Vol. 77, pp. 4243-4245.   In Swedish.

Akerstedt, T.   1976.   "Inter-individual differences in adjustment
to shift work", in Proceedings from the Sixth Congress of the
International Ergonomics Association.

---.   1979.   "Altered sleep/wake patterns and circadian rhythms:
Laboratory and field studies of sympathoadrenomedullary and
related variables", in Acta Physiologica Scandinavica, Supplement
469 (Stockholm).

---; Froberg, J.E.   1976.   "Shift work and health: Inter-
disciplinary aspects", in Rentos, P.G. and Shaphard, R.D. (eds.):
Shift work and health: A symposium, DHEW (NIOSH) Publication
No. 76-203, Washington, DC, US Government Printing Office.

---; ---.   1977.   "Psychophysiological circadian rhythms in
females during 75 hours of sleep deprivation with continuous
activity", in Waking and Sleeping, Vol. 4, pp. 387-394.

---; ---; Levi, L.; Torsvall, L.; Zamore, K.   1978.   Shift work
and well-being.   Stockholm, Arbetarskyddsnamnden.   In Swedish.

---; Levi, L.   1978.   "Circadian rhythms in the secretion of
cortisol, adrenaline and noradrenaline", in European Journal of
Clinical Investigation (Berlin), Vol. 8, pp. 57-58.

---; Theorell, T.   1976.   "Exposure to night work: Relations
between serum gastrin reactions, psychosomatic complaints and
personality variables", in Journal of Psychosomatic Research
(London), Vol. 20, pp. 479-484.

---; Torsvall, L. 1977a. "Experimental changes in shift schedules: Their effects on well-being", in Rutenfranz, J., Colquhoun, P., Kauth, P., and Folkards, S. (eds.): Proceedings of the IVth Symposium on Night and Shift Work, Dortmund.

---; ---. 1977b. Medical, psychological and social aspects of shift work at the Special Steel Mills in Soderfors, Reports from the Laboratory for Clinical Stress Research, No. 64, University of Stockholm. In Swedish.

---; ---. 1978. "Experimental changes in shift schedules: Their effects on well-being", in Ergonomics, Vol. 21, pp. 849-856.

Bainbridge, L. 1978. "The process controller", in Singleton, W.T. (ed.): The study of real skill, London, MTP Press.

Blauner, R. 1964. Alienation and freedom: The factory worker and his industry. Chicago, University of Chicago Press.

Blohmke, M.; Reimer, F. 1980. Krankheit und Beruf. Heidelberg, Dr. Alfred Hüthig Verlag.

Bolinder, E. 1974. Arbetsanpassning (Work adaptation). Praktisk information för skyddsombud m. fl. LO Informerar 4, Stockholm, Bokförlaget Prisma.

Bradbent, D.E. 1971. Decision and stress. New York, Academic Press.

Brod, J. 1971. "The influence of higher nervous processes induced by psychosocial environment on the development of essential hypertension", in Levi, L. (ed.): Society, stress and disease: The psychosocial environment and psychosomatic diseases, London, Oxford University Press, pp. 312-323.

Bronner, K.; Levi, L. 1973. Stress im Arbeitsleben. Göttingen, Musterschmidt.

Cohen, A. 1973. Industrial noise and medical absence and accident record data on exposed workers, Proceedings of the International Congress on Noise as a Public Problem, Dubrovnik, Yugoslavia.

Co-determination Act. 1976. The Swedish Code of Statutes, No. 580.

Cooper, C.L.; Payne, R. 1980. Current concerns in occupational stress. Chichester, John Wiley and Sons.

Denolin, H. (ed.) 1982. Psychological problems before and after myocardial infarction. Basel, S. Karger.

Dolan, S.; Arsenault, A. 1980. Stress, santé et rendement au travail. Ecole de Relations Industrielles, Université de Montréal, Monographie 5, Montréal.

Elliott, G.R.; Eisdorfer, C. 1982. Stress and human health. New York, Springer Publishing Company.

Forssman, S.; Coppée, G.H. 1975. Occupational health problems of young workers. Geneva, ILO.

Frankenhaeuser, M.   1976.   "The role of peripheral catecholamines in adaptation to understimulation and overstimulation", in Serban, G. (ed.): Psychopathology of human adaptation, New York, Plenum Press, pp. 173-191.

---.   1977a.   "Quality of life: Criteria for behavioural adjustment", in International Journal of Psychology, Vol. 12, pp. 99-100.

---.   1977b.   "Job demands, health and well-being", in Journal of Psychosomatic Research (London) Vol. 21, pp. 313-321.

---.   1977c.   Living in technified society: Stress tolerance and cost of adaptation.   Rapporteur, Psychological Institute, University of Stockholm, No. 15.   In Swedish.

---.   1979.   "Psychoneuroendocrine approaches to the study of emotion as related to stress and coping", Howe, H.E. and Dienstbier, R.A. (eds.): Nebraska Symposium on Motivation, Lincoln, University of Nebraska Press, pp. 123-161.

---.   1980a.   "Psychobiological aspects of life stress", in Levine, S. and Ursin, H. (eds.): Coping and health, New York, Plenum Press, pp. 203-223.

---.   1980b.   The human factor: An obstacle to safe nuclear power. Mimeograph, Stockholm.

---.   1981.   "Coping with job stress: A psychobiological approach", in Gardell, B. and Johansson, G. (eds.): Working life: A social science contribution to work reform, London, Wiley.

---; Gardell, B.   1976.   "Underload and overload in working life: Outline of a multidisciplinary approach", in Journal of Human Stress (Framingham), Vol. 2, pp. 35-46.

---; Johansson, G.   1976.   "Task demand as reflected in catecholamine excretion and heart rate", in Journal of Human Stress (Framingham), Vol. 2, pp. 15-23.

---; Lundberg, U.; Forsman, L.   1980.   "Dissociation between sympathetic-adrenal and pituitary-adrenal responses to an achievement situation characterised by high controllability: Comparison between Type A and Type B males and females", in Biological Psychology (Amsterdam), Vol. 10, pp. 79-91.

---; Rissler, A.   1970.   "Effects of punishment on catecholamine release and efficiency of performance", in Psychopharmacologia, Vol. 17, pp. 378-390.

Froberg, J.E.   1977.   "Twenty-four hour patterns in human performance, subjective and physiological variables and differences between morning and evening active subjects", in Biological Psychology (Amsterdam), Vol. 5, pp. 119-134.

---; Karlsson, C.G.; Levi, L.; Lidberg, L.   1975a.   "Circadian rhythms of catecholamine excretion, shooting range performance and self-ratings of fatigue during sleep deprivation", in Biological Psychology (Amsterdam), Vol. 2, pp. 175-188.

---; ---; ---; ---.   1975b.   "Psychobiological circadian rhythms during a 72-hour vigil", in Forsvarsmedicin, Vol. 11, pp. 192-201.

Gardell, B.   1971.   Technology, alienation and mental health: A sociopsychological study of industrial work, Stockholm, PA-Council. In Swedish.

---.   1976.   Job content and quality of life, Stockholm, Prisma. In Swedish.

---.   1979.   Work environment of white-collar workers: Psychosocial work environment and health, Working Paper, Department of Psychology, University of Stockholm.   In Swedish.

---.   1979.   "Psychosocial aspects of industrial production methods", in Reports from the Department of Psychology, University of Stockholm, Suppl. 47.

---.   1980.   Scandinavian research on stress in working life, Paper presented at the IRRA-Symposium on Stress in Working Life, Denver, Colorado, 5-7 Sep. 1980.

---;   Johansson, G.   1981.   Working life: A social science contribution to work reform.   Chichester, John Wiley and Sons.

Grandjean, E.   1969.   Fitting the task to the man.   London, Taylor and Francis Ltd.

Hamburg, D.A.; Nightingale, E.O.; Kalmar, V. (eds.).   1979. Healthy people: The surgeon general's report on health promotion and disease prevention.   Background papers, Washington, DC, US Government Printing Office, No. 79-55071A.

Henry, J.P.; Stephens, P.M.   1977.   Stress, health and the social environment.   New York, Springer-Verlag.

House, J.S.   1981.   Work stress and social support.   Reading, Addison-Wesley Pub. Co.

Hunt, V.R.   1975.   Occupational health problems of pregnant women. Washington, DC, US Department of Health, Education and Welfare (Order No. SA-5304-75.)

ILO.   1951.   Payment by results.   Geneva.

---.   1974a.   Migrant workers.   Report VII(1), International Labour Conference, 59th Session, Geneva.

---.   1974b.   Migrant workers.   Report VII(2), International Labour Conference, 59th Session, Geneva.

---.   1976a.   Making work more human: Working conditions and environment.   Report of the Director-General, International Labour Conference, 60th Session, Geneva.

---.   1976b.   Women workers and society: International perspectives.   Report of the Director-General, International Labour Conference, 60th Session, Geneva.

---.   1977a.   Protection of workers against noise and vibration in the working environment.   ILO Codes of Practice, Geneva.

---.   1977b.   Young people in their working environment.

Johansson, G. 1976. "Subjective well-being and temporal patterns of sympathetic adrenal medullary activity", in Biological Psychology (Amsterdam), Vol. 4, pp. 157-172.

---. 1979. "Psychoneuroendocrine reactions to mechanised and computerised work routines", in Mackay, C. and Cox, T. (eds.): Response to stress: Occupational aspects, London, IPC Science and Technology Press, pp. 142-149.

---; Aronsson, G. 1980. "Stress reactions in computerised administrative work", in Reports from the Department of Psychology, Suppl. 50, University of Stockholm.

---; ---; Lindstrom, B.O. 1979. "Social, psychological and neuro-endocrine stress reactions in highly mechanised work", in Ergonomics, Vol. 21, pp. 583-599.

---; Frankenhaeuser, M. 1973. "Temporal factors in sympatho-adrenomedullary activity following acute behavioural activation", in Biological Psychology (Amsterdam), Vol. 1, pp. 63-73.

---; Gardell, B. 1978. Psychosocial aspects of process control (Swedish), Rapporteur, Psychological Institute, University of Stockholm, No. 15.

Kagan, A.R.; Cederblad, M.; Hook, B.; Levi, L. 1978. "Evaluation of the effect of increasing the number of nurses on health and behaviour of 3-year old children in day care, satisfaction of their parents and health and satisfaction of their nurses", in Reports from the Laboratory for Clinical Stress Research, No. 89, University of Stockholm.

---; Levi, L. 1974. "Health and environment - Psychosocial stimuli: A review", in Social Science and Medicine (Oxford), Vol. 8, pp. 225-241.

Kahn, R.L. Work and health. 1981. New York, John Wiley and Sons.

Karasek, R.A. Jr. 1979. "Job demands, job decision latitude and mental strain: Implications for job redesign", in Administrative Science Quarterly, Vol. 24, pp. 285-308.

---. 1981. "Job socialisation and job strain: The implications of two related psychosocial mechanisms for job design", in Gardell, B. and Johansson, G. (eds.): Working life: A social science contribution to work reform, London, Wiley.

Kjellgren, O. 1975. Wage administrative study, Stockholm, LKAB. In Swedish.

Kornhauser, A. 1965. Mental health of the industrial worker. New York, Wiley.

Kronlund, J. 1974. Democracy without power, Stockholm, Prisma. In Swedish.

Lapin, B.A.; Cherkovich, G.M. 1971. "Environmental changes causing the development of neuroses and corticovisceral pathology in monkeys", in Levi, L. (ed.): Society, stress, and disease - The psychosocial environment and psychosomatic diseases, London, Oxford University Press, pp. 266-279.

Lazarus, R.S.   1966.   Psychological stress and the coping process. New York, McGraw-Hill Book Company.

---.   1976.   Patterns of adjustment.   Third edition, New York, McGraw-Hill Book Company.

Levi, L.   1964.   "The stress of everyday work as reflected in productiveness, subjective feelings, and urinary output of adrenaline and noradrenaline under salaried and piece-work conditions", in Journal of Psychosomatic Research (London), Vol. 8, pp. 199-202.

---.   1967.   Stress: Sources, management and prevention.   New York, Liveright.

---.   1970.   Vom Krankenbett zum Arbeitsplatz.   Zurich, Muster-schmidt.

---.   (ed.)   1971.   "Society, stress and disease", in The psycho-social environment and psychosomatic diseases, Vol. 1, London, Oxford University Press.

---.   1972.   "Stress and distress in response to psychosocial stimuli", in Acta Medica Scandinavica (Stockholm), 191, Suppl. 528.

---.   (ed.)   1975.   Emotions: Their parameters and measurement. New York, Raven Press.

---.   1976.   "Psychosocial conditions in the work environment: Effects on health and well-being", in Arbetsmiljoutredningens betankande, Bilage, Vol. 2, pp. 87-118.   In Swedish.

---.   (ed.)   1978.   "Society, stress and disease", in Male/female roles and relationships, Vol. 3, London, Oxford University Press.

---.   1979.   "Psychosocial factors in preventive medicine", in Hamburg, D.A., Nightingale, E.O. and Kalmar, V. (eds.): Healthy people: The surgeon general's report on health promotion and disease prevention, Background papers, Washington, DC, US Government Printing Office.

---.   (ed.)   1981a.   Society, stress and disease: Working life, Vol. IV, New York, Oxford University Press.

---.   1981b.   Preventing work stress.   Reading, Addison-Wesley.

---.   1981c.   "Prevention of stress-related disorders on a population scale", in International Journal of Mental Health, Vol. 9, No. 1-2. pp. 9-26.

---.   (ed.)   1984.   Society, stress and disease: Aging and old age.   Oxford, Oxford University Press.

---;   Andersson, L.   1975.   Psychosocial stress: Population, environment and quality of life.   New York, Spectrum Publications.

---;   ---.   1979.   Narodo-naselenije, okrushajushtshaja sreda i katshestwa shisni.   Moscow, Ekonomika Press.

---;   Frankenhaeuser, M;   Gardell, B.   1982.   "Work stress related to social structures and processes", in Elliott, G.R. and Eisdorfer, C. (eds.): Stress and human health, New York, Springer.

LO (Swedish Trade Union Confederation). 1980. Mental and social hazards to health in the working environment: Programme of action. Stockholm, LO.

Lohmann, H. 1978. Krankheit oder Entfremdung? Psychische Probleme in der Uberflussgesellschaft. Stuttgart, Georg Thieme Verlag.

Lundberg, U. 1976. "Urban commuting: Crowdedness and catecholamine excretion", in Journal of Human Stress (Framingham), Vol. 2, pp. 26-32.

---; Frankenhaeuser, M. 1978. "Psychophysiological reactions to noise as modified by personal control over noise intensity", in Biological Psychology, Vol. 6, pp. 51-59.

---; ---. 1980. "Pituitary-adrenal and sympathetic-adrenal correlates of distress and effort", in Journal of Psychosomatic Research (London), Vol. 24, pp. 125-130.

Mackay, C.; Cox. T. 1979. Response to stress: Occupational aspects. Guildford, Surrey, IPC Science and Technology Press.

McLean, A.A. 1979. Work stress. Reading, Addison-Wesley Publishing Company.

---; Black, G.; Colligan, M. (eds.). 1977. Reducing occupational stress. US Department of Health, Education and Welfare, National Institute for Occupational Safety and Health, Washington, DC.

Magnusson, M.; Nilsson, C. 1979. To work at inconvenient hours, Lund, Prisma. In Swedish.

Maule, H.G.; Levi, L.; McLean, A.; Pardon, N.; Savicev, M. 1973. Occupational mental health. Geneva, World Health Organisation.

Maurice, M. 1975. Shift work: Economic advantages and social costs. Geneva, ILO.

Meissner, M. 1971. "The long arm of the job: A study of work and leisure", in Industrial Relations, Vol. 10, pp. 238-260.

Mendelievich, E. (ed.). 1979. Children at work. Geneva, ILO.

Mjasnikov, A.L. 1961. Discussion in Proceedings of the Joint WHO-Czechoslovak Cardiological Society Symposium on the Pathogenesis of Essential Hypertension, Prague.

Moss, L. 1981. Management stress. Reading, Addison-Wesley Publishing Company.

National Board of Occupational Safety and Health. Mental and social aspects of the work environment, Stockholm, Arbetarskyddsstyrelsens forfattningssamling, AFS 1980:14. In Swedish.

National Swedish Board of Health and Welfare. 1978. Psykist halsovard 1 - forskning, social rapportering, dokumentation och information (Mental health protection and promotion 1 - Research, monitoring, documentation and information). Stockholm, Liber forlag.

Obrist, P.A. 1981. Cardio-vascular psychophysiology: A perspective. New York, Plenum Press.

Orth-Gomér, K; Olivegard-Landén, R. 1981. "Intervention on risk factors for coronary heart disease by changing working conditions of Swedish police officers", in Reports from the Laboratory for Clinical Stress Research, No. 126, University of Stockholm.

Polezhayev, Y.F.; Kalinina, N.P.; Makushin, V.G.; Slavina, S.E.; Dorosoychenko, V.I. 1974. Fiziolosicheskiye i psikholosicheskiye osnovy truda (Physiological and psychological foundations of work). Moscow, Profizdat Press.

Pöyhönen, M. 1975. Piece-rates and stress, Helsinki, Institute of Occupational Health, Report No. 115. In Swedish.

Raab, W. 1971. "Preventive myocardiology - Proposals for social action", in Levi, L. (ed.): Society, stress and disease - The psychosocial environment and psychosomatic diseases, London, Oxford University Press, pp. 389-394.

Rissler, A. 1978. "Stress reactions at work and after work during a period of quantitative overload", in Ergonomics, Vol. 20, pp.13-16.

Rodgers, G.; Standing, G. (eds.). 1981. Child work, poverty and underdevelopment. Geneva, ILO.

Rozwadowska-Dowzenko, M.; Kotlarska, H.; Zawadskj, M. 1956. "Nadcisrienie tetnicze samoistne a wykonywany zawod" ("Essential hypertension and profession"), in Polskie Archiwum Medycyny Wewnetrznej (Warszaw), Vol. 26, p. 497.

Salvendy, G.; Smith, M.J. (eds.). 1981. Machine pacing and occupational stress. London, Taylor and Francis Ltd.

SCA-tidningen. 1975. Monthly salaries in logging, Sundsvall, Sweden, No. 10. In Swedish.

Selye, H. 1971. "The evolution of the stress concept - Stress and cardiovascular disease", in Levi, L. (ed.): Society, stress and disease - The psychosocial environment and psychosomatic diseases, London, Oxford University Press, pp. 299-311.

Shalit, B. 1976. "Comparing the potentials and limitations of men and women, with emphasis on organisations", in Report No. 51 from the Laboratory for Clinical Stress Research, Stockholm.

Shostak, A.B. 1979. Blue-collar stress. Reading, Addison-Wesley Publishing Company.

Singer, J.E.; Lundberg, U.; Frankenhaeuser, M. 1978. "Stress on the train: A study of urban commuting", in Baum, A.; Singer, J.E.; and Valins, S. (eds.): Advances in environmental psychology. Vol. 1: The urban environment, Hillsdale, Lawrence Erlbaum Associates, pp. 41-56

Svensson, J.C., 1983: Early Stages of Essential Hypertension in a Psychosomatic Perspective - Epidemiological, Clinical, Psycho-physiological and Psychological Studies of 18-year-old Men. Doctoral Dissertation, Dept. of Psychology, University of Stockholm.

Swedish Forest Service. 1975. <u>One-year report on experiment with monthly salaries in logging</u>, Stockholm, Domanverket, mimeograph. In Swedish.

Swedish Secretariat for Futurological Studies. 1978. <u>Omsorgen i samhallet</u> (Societal care), Stockholm, Liber forlag.

Theorell, T.; Akerstedt, T. 1976. "Day and night work: Changes in cholesterol, uric acid, glucose and potassium in serum and in circadian patterns of urinary catecholamine excretion: A longitudinal cross-over study of railway workers", in <u>Acta Medica Scandinavica</u> (Stockholm), Vol. 200, pp. 47-53.

United States Surgeon General. 1979. <u>Healthy people</u>. Report on health promotion and disease prevention, United States Department of Health, Education and Welfare, DHEW (PHS) Publication No. 79-55071, Washington, DC.

Vester, F. 1976. <u>Phänomen Stress</u>. Stuttgart, Deutsche Verlagsanstalt.

Walker, C.R.; Guest, R.H. 1952. <u>The man on the assembly line</u>. Cambridge, Harvard University Press.

Warshaw, L.J. 1979. <u>Managing stress</u>. Reading, Addison-Wesley Publishing Company.

Weiner, H. 1979. <u>Psychobiology of essential hypertension</u>. New York, Elsevier.

Weiss, S.M.; Herd, J.A.; Fox, B.H. 1981. <u>Perspectives on behavioural medicine</u>. New York, Academic Press.

Westlander, G. 1976. <u>Working conditions and the content of leisure</u>. Stockholm, Swedish Council for Personnel Administration. In Swedish.

WHO. 1973. <u>Environmental and health monitoring in occupational health</u>. WHO Technical Report, Series No. 535.

___. 1976. "Occupational health problems and their control" in <u>WHO Chronicle</u>, Vol. 30, pp. 318-324.

Wilensky, H.L. 1981. "Family life cycle, work and the quality of life: Reflections on the roots of happiness, despair and indifference in modern society", in Gardell, B. and Johansson, G. (eds.): <u>Working life: A social science contribution to work reform</u>, London, Wiley.

Wolf, S. 1971. Psychosocial influences in gastro-intestinal function", in Levi, L. (ed.): <u>Society, stress and disease - The psychosocial environment and psychosomatic diseases</u>, London, Oxford University Press, pp. 362-366.

---. 1981. Social environment and health. Seattle, University of Washington Press.

---; Bruhn, J.G.; Goodell, H. 1978. Occupational health as human ecology. Springfield, Charles C. Thomas Pub.

---; Almy, T.P.; Bachrach, W.H.; Spiro, H.M.; Sturdevant, Weiner, H. 1979. "The role of stress in peptic ulcer disease", in Journal of Human Stress (Framingham), Vol. 5, No. 2, pp. 27-37.

Zdravomyslov, A.G.; Yadov, V.A. 1966. "Effect of vocational distinctions on the attitude to work", in Osipov, G.V. (ed.): Industry and labour in the USSR, London, Tavistock Pub., pp. 99-125.

Zwingmann, C.H.; Pfister-Ammende, M. (eds.). 1973. Uprooting and after ..., New York, Springer-Verlag.